TALES FROM MANY LANDS

An Anthology of Multicultural Folk Literature

Anita Stern

Adela Moron

National Textbook Company
a division of NTC/CONTEMPORARY PUBLISHING COMPANY
Lincolnwood, Illinois USA

Acknowledgments

"One More Child" adapted from "One More Child" from *The Beautiful Blue Jay and Other Tales of India* (Little, Brown, 1967) by John W. Spellman. Reprinted by permission of John W. Spellman.

"The Three Wishes" adapted from "The Three Wishes (Los Tres Deseos)" from *The Three Wishes: A Collection of Puerto Rican Folktales* (Harcourt, Brace, 1969) by Ricardo E. Alegría. Reprinted by permission of Ricardo E. Alegría.

"The Land of the Blue Faces" adapted from "The Land of the Blue Faces" from *The Flying Horses: Tales from China* (Methuen Children's Books, 1977) by Jo Manton and Robert Gittings. Reprinted by permission of Reed Consumer Books.

"Mr. Frog's Dream" adapted from "Mister Frog's Dream" from *Latin American Tales: From the Pampas to the Pyramids of Mexico* (Rand McNally, 1966) by Genevieve Barlow. Reprinted by permission of Eiko Tien, Conservator for the Estate of Genevieve Barlow: To my beloved friends, Tony, Barbara, & Eiko.

"The Blue Cat" adapted from "The Blue Cat" from *The Elephant's Bathtub* by Frances Carpenter. © 1962 by Frances Carpenter Huntington. Used by permission of Doubleday, a division of Bantam Doubleday Dell Publishing Group, Inc.

"The Little Orphan" adapted from "The Little Orphan" from *Turkish Fairy Tales* (Van Nostrand, 1964) by Selma Ekrem. Reprinted by permission of Wadsworth Publishing Co.

"Why the Monsoon Comes Each Year" adapted from "Why the Monsoon Comes Each Year" from *Fairy Tales from Vietnam* (Dodd, Mead, 1968) retold by Dorothy Lewis Robertson. Reprinted by permission of Dorothy L. Robertson.

"The Tortoise Wins a Race" adapted from "Jabotí, the Tortoise, Wins a Race" from *Adventures of Jabotí on the Amazon* (Abelard-Schuman, 1968) by Lena F. Hurlong. Reprinted by permission of Edmond Hurlong, Conservator for the Estate of Lena F. Hurlong.

"The Lazy Fox" adapted from "The Lazy Fox" from *Latin American Tales: From the Pampas to the Pyramids of Mexico* (Rand McNally, 1966) by Genevieve Barlow. Reprinted by permission of Eiko Tien, Conservator for the Estate of Genevieve Barlow: To my beloved friends, Tony, Barbara, & Eiko.

"The Giant Bird" adapted from "Oni and the Great Bird" from *Fourteen Hundred Cowries & Other African Tales* (© Oxford University Press 1962) by Abayomi Fuja. Reprinted by permission of Oxford University Press.

"The Man Who Lived a Thousand Years" adapted from "The Man Who Lived a Thousand Years" from *Tales of a Korean Grandmother* (Doubleday, 1947) by Frances Carpenter. Reprinted by permission of Edith H. Williams, Conservator for the Estate of Frances Carpenter Huntington.

"The Princess of the Golden Island" adapted from "Majka" from *The Jolly Tailor and Other Fairy Tales Translated from the Polish* (Longman, Green, 1928) by Lucia Merecka Borski. Reprinted by permission of Edmond Temple, Executor for the Borski Trust.

"The Frogs and the Grubs" adapted from "The Legend of the Dragon-fly and the Frogs" from *Legends from the Outback* (J. M. Dent, 1958) by Phyllis M. Power. Reprinted by permission of The Orion Publishing Group.

"The Great Peace" adapted from "The Great Peace" from *Thunder in the Mountains* by Hilda Mary Hooke. © Oxford University Press Canada, 1947. Reprinted by permission of Oxford University Press Canada.

"David and the Spider" adapted from "David and the Spider" from *Fairy Tales from Grandfather's Big Book: Jewish Legends of Old Retold for Young People* (Behrman House, 1949) by Edith Lindeman Colisch. Reprinted by permission of Behrman House.

"The Sleeping Princess" adapted from "The Sleeping Princess" from *Of the Night Wind's Telling: Legends from the Valley of Mexico* by E. Adams Davis. Drawings by Dorothy Kirk. © 1946 by the University of Oklahoma Press. Reprinted by permission of the University of Oklahoma Press.

"The Giants and the Dwarfs" adapted from "The Giants and the Dwarfs" from *Tales Told in Holland* (The Book House for Children, 1926) by Olive Beaupré Miller. © The United Educators, Inc. Reprinted by permission of The United Educators, Inc.

Cover Illustration: Diane Novario
Interior Illustrations: Marcy Ramsey

ISBN: 0-8442-0855-8

Published by National Textbook Company,
a division of NTC/Contemporary Publishing Company,
4255 West Touhy Avenue,
Lincolnwood (Chicago), Illinois 60646-1975 U.S.A.
© 1996 by NTC/Contemporary Publishing Company

In loving memory of
my grandparents, Sophie and Nathan Goodman,
my Buba and Zada,
who always had a story for me

CONTENTS

TO THE READER

In *Tales from Many Lands* you will read stories from many countries in the world. Before you read each story you will learn something about the country or culture the story comes from. The activities before and after each story will help you understand the story and learn to read, write, and speak English better.

This reading book is fun! You'll laugh when you read some stories. You'll be surprised by the endings of other stories. You will be sad when you finish a few of them. You will want to finish each story to find out what happens.

All the stories are tied together by one idea: the choices people make in life. This book looks at three kinds of choices: looking for happiness, trying to win, and getting along with others. These are choices that all of us make.

P A R T   O N E

LOOKING *for* HAPPINESS

C
One More Child

INDIAN

The history of India began about 4,500 years ago. It was always a very important country in southern Asia. It was famous for its wonderful buildings, jewelry, rugs, and spices. Today India is the second-largest country in the world in population. Its people speak many different languages. Hindi and English are the main languages of India.

Before You Read

Talk about the following.
1. Look at the picture for this story. Describe the poor woman and her children, their clothes, and their house.
2. Describe the other woman and what she is holding.
3. Guess why the other woman is visiting this family.

Practicing New Words

You will find these words in the story. Study their meanings.

bowl   deep dish for soup or other food

enough   as much as needed

(to) feed   to give food to people or animals

(to) give away   to give a person something that belongs to you

hole   an opening in something

neighbor   a person living or sitting near you

(to) wish   to want something very much

Fill in the blanks with the new words. Use each word only once.

1. I have a new _ neighbor _ living next door to me.
2. The supermarket will _ feed _ free eggs to everyone today.
3. Here is a small _ bowl _ for your ice cream.
4. Blow out the candles and _ wish _ for something you want.
5. I will _ feed _ the dog now.
6. The air is coming out of the balloon. It has a _ hole _ in it.
7. We have _ enough _ food for six people tonight.

One More Child

Once upon a time there was a very rich woman. She had beautiful clothes and a big house. She had no children, so she was very sad.

She asked a friend, "How can I get a child?"

Her friend told her, "Go to your poor neighbor. She has twelve children. She and her husband do not have enough money to feed all their children. Maybe she will give you one of her children. You are rich. You can feed the child much better than she can."

The rich woman asked her friend, "Do you think she will give away a child?"

Her friend answered, "Why not? Give her a bag of gold. I know she will give you a child."

The next day the rich woman took a bag of gold to the poor woman's little house. The poor woman was surprised to see her. She said, "Come in and sit down."

The children came to their mother and cried, "Please give us food. We are hungry."

The mother brought rice soup for the children. The poor family had no bowls. She put the soup in twelve holes in the floor. The children ate. Then the hungry mother ate the rice water they left in the holes.

The mother looked up and said, "Oh, God! Please give me one more child. Then I will have one more hole of rice water to eat from."

The rich woman watched quietly. She was surprised to hear the poor woman wish for one more child. She thought, "This woman will never give away any of her children."

She put the bag of gold in the poor woman's hand and left the little house. She was sad because she had no child. Now she understood a mother's love for her children.

Understanding the Story

A. What Happens?

Choose **a, b,** or **c** to complete each sentence.

1. The rich woman is sad because
    a. she has nobody to marry.
    b. her husband left her.
    c. she has no children.

2. She thinks the poor woman will give her a child because
    a. she doesn't have time to take care of so many children.
    b. she and her husband can't feed so many children.
    c. she loves gold, so she will give away a child to get some.

3. The poor woman
    a. wants God to give her one more child.
    b. wants to give away one of her children.
    c. wants the rich woman to leave her house.

4. The rich woman
    a. gives the mother some gold and takes one child.
    b. gives the mother nothing and doesn't take a child.
    c. gives the mother some gold but doesn't take a child.

B. Telling the Story Again

Fill in the blanks. Use the words you learned in **Practicing New Words**.

Once upon a time a poor woman did not have _____ food to _____ all of her hungry children. They had no _____s. The poor children ate from ___hole___s in the floor. A rich ___woman___ came to visit them. She hoped her poor neighbor wanted to ___give___ one child for a bag of gold. The rich woman was surprised when the poor woman said, "I _____ for one more child."

C. Looking Back

Answer these questions.

1. Why is the rich woman sad? *Because she doesn't has children*
2. Why does the rich woman's friend think the poor woman will give away a child? *Because the poor woman doesn't has money and feed for her children.*
3. What do the mother and children eat?
4. Why does the mother want one more child? *Because she will has one more hope of rice and water to eat from*
5. The rich woman doesn't get a child from the poor mother. Why does she give her the bag of gold?
6. What does the rich woman learn from the poor woman? *mother's love*
7. What do you think about the poor woman's wish? *for her children.*

Exploring the Meaning

A. Understanding What Rich Is

Complete the chart. Then answer the question.

Time	Character	She Has	She Doesn't Have
beginning of story	rich woman	*lots of money*	*a child*
beginning of story	poor woman	*twelve children*	*money and feed for her chil-dren.*
end of story	rich woman	*money*	*the children*
end of story	poor woman	*money*	*the children*

Do you think it is better to have lots of money or lots of children? Why?

B. Thinking About the Story

Finish these sentences.

1. The children in this story are _poor, hungry._.
2. The mother wants to ____care____ her children better, but she can't because _she is poor and she doesn't has #_
3. The rich woman is sad because _she doesn't has child_.
4. She is surprised when _The poor_____.
5. The rich woman learns that the poor woman will not _interesting_____, even for gold.
6. At the end of the story the rich woman is sad because _she doesn't have de children_.
7. The poor woman is happy because _she has her children and the love of them_.

C. In Everyday Life

Talk about these questions.

1. In what ways is it good to have many children?
2. In what ways is it good to have one or two children?
3. In what ways is it good to have no children?
4. Do children bring happiness to their parents? If so, how?
5. Do you want to have children someday? Why or why not?

Mr. Rabbit

NATIVE AMERICAN

Hundreds of Native American tribes lived in the Americas before the first Europeans explored the New World. Each tribe had its own language, way of life, and leader. This story comes from the Eastern Woodland area of what is now the United States. The Woodland Indians hunted and fished for their food and grew many kinds of vegetables. Telling stories was an important part of their life. These stories are still told by Native Americans today.

Before You Read

Talk about these questions.

1. Why are Native Americans sometimes called *Indians*? Which name do you think they like better? Why?
2. What do you know about Native American life in the eastern part of the United States?
3. What problems did the Native Americans have after Europeans came to the New World?

Practicing New Words

You will find these words in the story. Study their meanings.

(to) be yourself	to do things your way
(to) choke	not to be able to get air
(to) drown	to die in the water
eel	a long fish that looks like a snake
forest	many trees in one place
icy	full of ice; very cold
otter	a furry animal that lives near water, has ducklike feet, and eats fish

Fill in the blanks with the new words. Use each word only once.

1. Watch your children near the swimming pool, so they do not ___drown___.

2. The ___forest___ is full of beautiful trees, plants, and wild animals.

3. The fisherman made a hole in the ___icy___ water to catch fish inside the river.

4. An ___otter___ is a furry animal that swims well.

5. An ___eel___ is long and thin and lives in salty or fresh water.

6. Always remember to think for yourself and ___be yourself___, because you are special.

7. Don't talk when you are eating fish, so you will not ___choke___ on the little bones.

Mr. Rabbit

A long time ago Mr. Rabbit lived with his grandmother in the forest. It was winter. The lakes and rivers were frozen. There was snow on all the fields. Mr. Rabbit worked very hard to find food for himself and his grandmother.

One day he was near a river. He saw the home of an otter. "Welcome," said the otter to Mr. Rabbit. "Will you have dinner with me?"

The otter went down an icy path to the river. Down he went into the water. He returned very quickly with some eels. He put them on the fire to cook. The rabbit and the otter ate a delicious meal.

"What a cheap and easy way the otter has to get food! I think I can do the same thing," Mr. Rabbit thought. He invited the otter to eat with him in three days.

Mr. Rabbit moved his home to the side of a lake. He made an icy path down to the water. He wanted to do just what the otter did. Three days later the otter arrived at Mr. Rabbit's house. Mr. Rabbit asked his grandmother, "Will you please cook dinner?"

"What will I cook?" she asked.

"I'll get something," said Mr. Rabbit.

Mr. Rabbit went down the path and jumped into the icy water. It felt very cold! But that was not the only problem. Mr. Rabbit did not know how to swim. He could not breathe in the water.

"What is the matter with the rabbit?" asked the otter.

The old grandmother was surprised, too. "I guess he saw someone do something. Now he is trying to do the same thing."

"Mr. Rabbit!" shouted the otter. "Come out of the water. I'll catch the fish."

The poor rabbit had no choice. He was choking and beginning to drown. He climbed out of the lake.

The otter jumped into the water. A few minutes later he came out with some eels. He told Mr. Rabbit, "Don't feel bad. But remember to be yourself. Don't try to catch any more eels!"

Understanding the Story

A. What Happens?

Match the sentence parts. Write the correct letter in each blank.

__d__ 1. Mr. Rabbit lives		a. in the icy water.
__g/f__ 2. The otter cooks		b. eels in the icy lake.
__e__ 3. The lake is		c. he can do anything.
__a__ 4. Mr. Rabbit almost drowns		d. with his grandmother.
__c__ 5. Mr. Rabbit thinks		e. icy cold.
__b__ 6. Mr. Rabbit cannot catch		f. eels for dinner.
__f__ 7. The otter quickly		g. catches some eels.

B. Telling the Story Again

Fill in the blanks. Use the words you learned in **Practicing New Words**.

Mr. Rabbit lived in a ___forest___ with his grandmother. In the winter he worked hard to find food. One winter day he visited his friend, an ___otter___. The otter caught some ___eel___s in an ___icy___ river. Mr. Rabbit thought it looked easy to get food that way.

The otter came to visit him a few days later. Mr. Rabbit jumped into a lake and tried to catch some eels. He ___choke___d and started to ___drown___ in the cold water. The rabbit got out of the water safely, but he did not catch any eels. The otter told him, "Remember to ___be yourself___."

C. Looking Back

Answer these questions.

1. Why was it hard for Mr. Rabbit to get food in the winter?
2. What did the otter and the rabbit eat?
3. How did the otter get the eels?
4. Why did Mr. Rabbit want to catch eels?
5. What happened to Mr. Rabbit in the water?
6. What did the otter tell Mr. Rabbit? Why?

Exploring the Meaning

A. Comparing Animals

Complete the chart. Then answer the questions.

Characteristics	Rabbits	Otters
Where do they live?	*in forests and on farms*	*near water*
What do they eat?	*plants*	*eat fish*
Can they swim?	*no*	*yes*
Can they easily catch fish?	*he can't no*	*yes he can*

How are rabbits and otters the same? How are they different?

B. Thinking About the Story

Finish these sentences.

1. An otter can easily catch eels
   because _he can swim_.
2. It was a mistake for Mr. Rabbit to try to catch eels
   because _he can't swim_.
3. Mr. Rabbit tried to do the same thing the otter did because it
   looked _it was easy to do._.
4. Mr. Rabbit learned that what is easy for someone may
   be _hard for others._.

C. In Everyday Life

Talk about these questions.

1. An *expert* is someone who knows a lot about something or is very good at something. Why does an expert's work often look easy?
2. When is it a good idea to try to copy an expert?
3. When is it wrong to try to copy an expert?
4. What should we understand about ourselves?

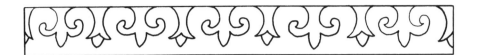

The Three Wishes

PUERTO RICAN

Puerto Rico is a Caribbean island southeast of Florida. It is a commonwealth of the United States: it is American land, but it is not a state. The native people of Puerto Rico are the Arawak Indians. People from Spain began moving to Puerto Rico in the 1500s. Today the main language of Puerto Rico is Spanish.

Before You Read

Talk about these questions.

1. What is one wish you have? Share your wish with other students in your class or group.
2. What kinds of wishes do people in your family have?
3. When do you make wishes (for example, on your birthday or when you see a star in the sky)?

Practicing New Words

You will find these words in the story. Study their meanings.

(to) come true	to happen
(to) disappear	to not be seen anymore
foolish	silly; not intelligent
gift	a present
(to) share	to give a part of what you have to others
(to) shout	to speak loudly
(to) test	to examine
(to) waste	to use in a silly way
wish	a hope that something will happen
woodsman	a man who cuts down trees for wood

Fill in the blanks with the new words. Use each word only once.

1. I want to give you a _____gift_____ for your birthday.
2. We have only a few books, so please _____share_____ them.
3. The _____woodsman_____ cut down many trees yesterday.
4. After many years of war, we all have one _____wish_____: peace.
5. The food will _____disappear_____ quickly when the people sit down to eat.
6. The drivers began to _____shout_____ at each other about the accident.
7. Be careful not to say anything _____foolish_____ when you are angry.
8. Wars _____test_____ what people will do in emergencies.
9. Don't _____waste_____ your money on that!
10. I hope that your wish will _____come true_____ today!

The Three Wishes

Once upon a time a woodsman and his wife lived in a little house in the forest. They were poor but very happy. They loved each other very much. They were always ready to share everything they had with anyone who came to their door.

One day the woodsman was working in the forest. His wife was working at home. An old man came to their little house. He said he was very hungry. The woman had only a little food, but she shared it with him.

The old man ate. Then he said, "God sent me to test you. You and your husband share everything you have with everyone. God wants to give you a special gift because you are so kind."

"What is the gift?" asked the woman.

The old man answered, "You and your husband can make any three wishes and they will come true."

The woman was very happy. She said, "I wish my husband could be here to hear you!" In a minute her husband was there. Her first wish came true.

"What happened?" asked the woodsman. "I was in the forest. Why am I here now?" His wife kissed him and explained.

The woodsman listened to her story. Then he became angry. He shouted at his wife for the first time. "You wasted one of our wishes. Now we have only two left. You are so foolish! I wish you had donkey ears!"

His wife's ears began to grow. They changed into big donkey ears. The woman touched her long ears and cried. Her husband felt very bad about what he said.

The old man said, "You never shouted at each other before. Now you are different. You know you can have power and be rich. You have one wish left. Do you want to be rich? Do you want to have beautiful clothes?"

19

The woodsman said, "We only want to be happy again, like before."

The donkey ears disappeared. The woodsman and his wife thanked God. They were happy again.

The old man said, "Poor people can be very happy and rich people can be very unhappy. God will give you the biggest happiness a married couple can have."

A few months later the woodsman and his wife had a baby. The family lived happily ever after.

Understanding the Story

A. *When Does It Happen?*

Put these sentences in the correct order. Write **1** next to the sentence that tells what happened first.

___7___ The donkey ears disappeared.

___8___ The woodsman and his wife had a baby.

___4___ The woodsman got angry at his wife.

___1___ An old man came to the woodsman's house.

___6___ The woodsman wished to be happy again.

___3___ The woman wished for her husband to be there.

___2___ The old man said they had three wishes.

___5___ The woman grew donkey ears.

B. *Telling the Story Again*

Fill in the blanks. Use the words you learned in **Practicing New Words**.

A _woodsman_ and his wife were very happy together. They liked to _share_ what they had with other people.

One day an old man came to their house. He told the woman that God had a _gift_ for her and her husband. He said that she and her husband could make three _wish_es. He told her, "They will _come true_."

The woman got excited and made a _____*foolish*_____ wish because she didn't think carefully. Then the woodsman started to _____*shout*_____ at her and wished she had donkey ears. They _____*dissappear*___ed when the woodsman wished to be happy again with his wife.

The couple had a baby a few months later. The family was very happy.

C. Looking Back

Answer these questions.

1. Why did the old man come to the couple's house? *he came to test them and he was hungry.*
2. What gift did he have for the woodsman and his wife? *3 wishes*
3. What did the woodsman and his wife wish for? *be happy.*
4. How did the wishes change the woodsman and his wife?
5. What was the second gift God gave the couple? *I wish you have donki ear.*

Exploring the Meaning

A. Making Wishes

Complete the chart. Then answer the question.

Wish Number	Who Made the Wish	What Was the Wish?	What Changed?
one	*the woman*	*Her husband could be there.*	*He shouted at her.*
two	*the man*	*Her wife could be donkey*	*Her wife ear*
three	*the man*	*He wished be Happy*	*Hear ear of Her wife.*

What should people do before they make wishes?

B. *Thinking About the Story*

Finish these sentences.

1. At the beginning of the story the woodsman and his wife were happy because _____.

2. The three wishes were a test to see _____.

3. The woodsman was angry at his wife because _____.

4. He wished she had donkey ears because _____.

5. The woodsman and his wife changed because the wishes _____.

6. The last wish was _____.

7. The woodsman and his wife did not wish for riches because _____.

C. *In Everyday Life*

Talk about these questions.

1. Why don't riches always bring people happiness?

2. What makes you happy?

3. Are poor people always unhappy? Why or why not?

4. What makes you unhappy?

The Old Father

RUSSIAN

Russia is the largest country in the world in land area. Part of Russia is in Asia and part of it is in Europe. From 1917 to 1991 Russia was the biggest part of the Soviet Union. Today it is in the Commonwealth of Independent States.

Before You Read

Talk about the following.

1. What do you know about life in Russia? What do you know about the weather in Russia?
2. Look at the picture of the old man. Describe him. Guess how he feels.
3. Guess what the old man is talking about to the younger man.

Practicing New Words

You will find these words in the story. Study their meanings.

carriage	a beautiful wagon for people to travel in
(to) feel sorry for	to feel bad about someone with a problem
(to) fool	to make someone believe something that is not true; to trick
(to) hide	to put in a secret place (past: **hid**)
knapsack	a bag for food and other things, often carried on the back
(to) shake	to move back and forth (past: **shook**)
treasure	something very valuable

Fill in the blanks with the new words. Use each word only once.

1. Some parents like to ___hide___ their children's presents until their birthdays.
2. The young man put his ___knapsack___ on his back and walked away.
3. I ___feel sorry for___ Nick. He can't find a good job.
4. Remember to ___shake___ the medicine before you take it.
5. That tricky man knows how to ___fool___ people. They give him money and get nothing for it.
6. The princess rode in a ___carriage___ pulled by eight white horses.
7. There are many boxes of ___treasure___ at the bottom of the sea because many pirate ships went down into the ocean.

The Old Father

Once upon a time there was an old man. He had four sons. They grew up, and the old man gave everything he had to them. "I will live with my children the rest of my days," he thought.

The oldest son said, "We must give our father food and clothes. We must take care of him and make him happy."

At first the oldest son and his family took good care of the old man. After some time passed the son did not want to keep his old father in his house. He shouted at him. He stopped taking good care of him.

Life got very bad for the old father. He went to his second son. Life was no better there. Every time he ate, his son and his son's wife were angry. The old man went to the next son. He went to all four sons. Every son said, "We cannot keep you."

The old man didn't know where to go. The four sons decided to send their father to a school in the next village. "At school he will have a place to sit," they said. "And he can take something to eat in his knapsack." The old man cried. He did not want to go to school. He was too old.

His sons sent him away through the forest. On the way he met a rich man riding in a carriage. The rich man asked him, "Where are you going?" The old man cried and told him the sad story of his life.

The rich man felt sorry for the old man. He said, "Don't go to school. I have a plan." He filled a bag with something. Then he said to the old man, "Take this bag home and tell your sons this story:

'My children, long ago I hid this bag of money in the forest. I did not touch it for many years. Now I found it again. I will keep it until I die. After I die, decide together who took care

26

of me the best. That son will get the biggest part of this money. Now, will you be kind to your old father—for money?'''

The old man took the bag and returned to his children. He told them the story.

Then all four brothers were very kind to their father. They took good care of him. The old man was happy. But he never went anyplace without the bag.

Finally the old man died. The children gave him a beautiful funeral. Then they hurried to get the money in the bag. Because all of the sons were good to their father, they decided to divide the money into four equal parts.

They shook the bag. Something was inside. It was a treasure! They opened it.

The bag was full of glass! They couldn't believe their eyes. They looked carefully. There was no money in the bag, only glass.

The people of the village laughed at them. "You sent your father to school," they said. "He learned something there. He learned to fool you!"

The sons were very angry and sad. But what could they do? Their father was already dead and buried.

Understanding the Story

A. What Happens?

Choose **a, b,** or **c** to complete each sentence.

1. The old man decided
   a. to give everything he had to his children.
   b. to keep everything he had for himself.
   c. to share what he had with his children.

2. The oldest son and his family
   a. always took good care of the old father.
   b. took good care of the old father at first, but then stopped.
   c. never took good care of the old father.

3. All four sons and their families decided to
    a. send their father away to another country.
    b. send their father to a home for poor people.
    c. send their father to the school in the next village.

4. The old man returned with a bag of money and said, "After I die,
    a. the son that took care of me the best will get most of this money."
    b. nobody will get this money."
    c. divide this money equally among you."

5. When the old man died, his sons opened the bag. They found
    a. nothing but glass in the bag.
    b. a treasure in the bag.
    c. money in the bag.

B. *Telling the Story Again*

Fill in the blanks. Use the words you learned in **Practicing New Words**.

Once upon a time there was an old man in Russia. He gave his four sons all his money. He lived with each son's family for a short time. Then the four sons told him to take his _____ and go to school in the next village.

   In the forest he met a rich man riding in a _____. The old man told him about his problems with his children. The rich man said, "I _____ you." He gave the old man a bag with something in it. Then he said, "Go to your children. Tell them you _____ a bag of money in the forest a long time ago. Say, 'I found my bag of money. When I die, please give most of the money in the bag to the son who took care of me the best.'" The old man did what the rich man said. His sons took good care of him.

   When the old man died, his sons wanted to see what was in the bag. They were sure the bag had a _____ in it. They _____ the bag and heard something inside. But they found only glass inside. The old man knew how to _____ his children.

C. Looking Back

Answer these questions.

1. Did the sons take good care of their father? Explain.
2. Where did the four sons send their father?
3. What did the rich man give the old man?
4. What did he tell the old man to say to his children?
5. What did the sons do after they saw the bag?
6. What was in the bag?

Exploring the Meaning

A. In the Family

Complete the chart. Then answer the questions.

Character(s)	What He/They Had	What He/They Said
the father	his life's savings	Take care of me.
the sons		We'll take care of you.
the sons	knapsack	
the rich man		Tell your sons this story.
the sons	a bag filled with glass	

Why did the sons trick their father? Why did the father trick his sons?

B. *Thinking About the Story*

Finish these sentences.

1. The father gave his sons everything he had because

   _____.

2. The sons sent their father to school because

   _____.

3. The man in the forest was rich, but he

   _____.

4. The sons started to take care of their father when

   _____.

5. They were disappointed when

   _____.

C. *In Everyday Life*

Talk about these questions.

1. Why do many adult children take care of their old parents?
2. Why do some adult children choose not to take care of their old parents?
3. What problems can an old parent bring to a family?
4. How is a home better when an old parent is part of the family?

The Land of the Blue Faces

CHINESE

China is the largest country in Asia. It has the largest population in the world. China has a history of about four thousand years. Many Chinese ideas about religion, art, science, and language passed into Korea, Japan, and other Asian countries when the Chinese emperors built very large empires.

Before You Read

Talk about these questions.

1. How can people have "blue faces"?
2. What do you know about life in China?
3. Look at the picture for this story. What do you think will happen?

Practicing New Words

You will find these words in the story. Study their meanings.

blanket	a large covering used to stay warm
(to) bow	to show respect by bending down
dragon	a large, imaginary reptile with wings and lion's feet
empress	wife of an emperor
gate	a door in a fence or wall
homesick	lonely for home; missing family and friends
roof	the top of a house
✓ **servant**	a worker who helps a person or helps in a house
shoulder	the top of the arm and the back
valley	a low place between mountains

Fill in the blanks with the new words. Use each word only once.

1. The princess called her ___servent___ to help her dress for the wedding.

2. The emperor sat next to his wife, the _____.

3. The servant covered the sleeping princess with a _____.

4. The cowboy opened the _____ and the horses ran out.

5. The _____ of the house was old, so rain came inside.

6. When people leave home, they sometimes feel _____.

7. The donkey walked slowly down the mountain to the _____.

8. I read a story about a giant and a _____.

9. The man carried his son on his _____s.

10. Everyone has to _____ down to the king.

The Land of the Blue Faces

The little princess cried. "I don't want to marry and go to the Land of the Blue Faces."

"A daughter of the Dragon Emperor should not cry this way," said her mother, the empress. "Wives cannot choose their husbands. I did not choose your father!"

The emperor came in with a shiny red box. "My lucky daughter, these gifts are from the man you will marry, the Lord of Tibet." He took a beautiful comb out of the box. The princess didn't look at it.

The little princess threw herself in front of her father and cried, "Please do not send me to the Land of the Blue Faces. I want to stay here with you. The people of Tibet paint their faces blue. They do not have beds or chairs. They even drink milk. I can never do that!"

The day came to leave. The little princess was a Chinese bride. She wore a red coat and a big red hat. She said good-bye to her parents and her home. Then she stepped into a chair with closed curtains. The servants carried her away.

They carried her through fields and forests, along rivers, and across a desert. The little princess was very sad. She did not open the curtains to look out. She sat and thought about the past. After many weeks they came to the mountains. They climbed higher and higher. The little princess was cold under her warm blankets. The wind was so loud she could not sleep. Then the road began to go down the mountains.

One morning the servants said, "This is the Land of the Blue Faces." The princess saw a valley filled with trees and beautiful fields. There was a shining river in the middle. The road went through a village. The people bowed when she passed. The princess saw they had brown, smiling faces. They looked like the Chinese farmers at home! The children waved to her. The princess smiled at them.

The road went on. Soon the princess saw the walls of a city. The roofs of many houses were blue and red and green. They were just like the roofs of the Chinese houses at home. The princess was surprised that everything looked so much like China.

"What will the Lord of Tibet look like?" she thought. "I think he will be old and ugly. Maybe he will have no teeth left."

The gates of the city opened. Many people came out. They wore Chinese clothes. They bowed and waved. They shouted in Chinese, "Long live the Lady of Tibet!"

A young man on a horse took off his hat and bowed to her. His face was brown, and his eyes were shining and happy. "Welcome to Tibet," he said.

"Is this really the Land of the Blue Faces?" asked the princess.

"Yes," he answered.

"But where are the people with blue faces?"

"The Lord of Tibet thought you would be afraid, so he sent them away."

"Why is this city full of Chinese buildings?"

"The Lord of Tibet was afraid you would be homesick, so he built this copy of a Chinese city for you."

"But the people are wearing Chinese clothes and speaking Chinese."

"The Lord of Tibet was afraid you would be homesick, so he told his people to copy the Chinese in everything."

"Please tell the Lord of Tibet I said 'thank you,'" said the princess.

The young man on the horse laughed. "I am the Lord of Tibet. We waited a long time for you to come, dear little princess. Now you are here, and the people want to see you. Will you ride into the city with me?"

The princess was very happy. She could never ride a horse at home. The Lord of Tibet helped her get on his horse. She held his strong shoulders.

A bride must leave her father's home sadly. The princess tried to look a little sad, but in her heart she was very happy. She was the Lady of Tibet, in the Land of the Blue Faces.

Understanding the Story

A. What Happens?

Match the sentence parts. Write the correct letter in each blank.

_____ 1. The princess didn't want   a. a red coat and a red hat.

_____ 2. The empress told   b. on the horse with the Lord of Tibet.

_____ 3. The princess wore   c. that the Lord of Tibet was old and ugly.

_____ 4. The servants carried   d. young and strong.

_____ 5. The princess was surprised   e. to see the people with blue faces.

_____ 6. The princess was worried   f. the princess to Tibet.

_____ 7. The Lord of Tibet was   g. her daughter not to cry.

_____ 8. The princess sat   h. that everything looked like China.

B. Telling the Story Again

Fill in the blanks. Use the words you learned in **Practicing New Words**.

The _____ told her daughter not to be sad. She must go to the Land of the Blue Faces. The _____ Emperor said good-bye to his daughter. A _____ helped the princess get into her chair. Then the servants carried her to Tibet.

    It was cold, so the princess covered herself with a warm _____. They passed over the mountains and came to a beautiful _____. Then the princess saw a city. The houses had red, green, and blue _____s.

The _____s opened. A young man on a horse came to meet the princess.

    The princess was surprised that he was the Lord of Tibet. She rode with him on his horse, holding his strong _____s with her hands. She was very happy!

C. Looking Back

Answer these questions.

1. Why didn't the princess want to go to Tibet?
2. What did the empress tell her daughter about marriage?
3. What did the servants cross on the way to Tibet?
4. Why was the princess surprised when she came to Tibet?
5. Why was she happy at the end of the story?

Exploring the Meaning

A. Surprises

Complete the chart. Then answer the question.

Life in Tibet	The Princess Expected	The Princess Found
the faces	*blue faces*	*brown faces*
the language	Tibetan	
the clothes	Tibetan	
the houses		Chinese
the Lord of Tibet		young and strong

Why was the princess so happy to be in Tibet?

B. Thinking About the Story

Finish these sentences.

1. The princess didn't want to go to Tibet because
   _____.

2. She had to go because _____.

3. She was surprised that _____.

4. The Lord of Tibet made the changes so that
   _____.

5. At the end she felt happy because
   _____.

C. In Everyday Life

Talk about these questions.

1. In your country, do young people choose the person they will marry? If not, who chooses?

2. Do you think you or your parents should choose the person you will marry?

3. What are some good reasons to marry a person from your own country?

4. What are some good reasons to marry a person from a different country?

Mr. Frog's Dream

NICARAGUAN

Nicaragua is the largest Central American country in land area. Its people are mostly farmers. Their way of life comes from both their Indian history and the Spanish who came to their land. The main language of Nicaragua is Spanish.

Before You Read

Talk about the following.
1. Do you know any stories about frogs? If so, share one with the class.
2. Look at the picture for this story. Guess what the large frog is telling the other frogs.
3. Try to remember a dream you had. What do you think your dream means?

Practicing New Words

You will find these words in the story. Study their meanings.

dizzy   a feeling in your head that everything is moving, but it is not

(to) float   to ride on top of water or air

mud   wet, soft earth

pond   a small lake

Fill in the blanks with the new words. Use each word only once.

1. A piece of paper will _____ on water.
2. Clean your shoes so you don't bring _____ into the house.
3. I hit my head, and now I feel _____.
4. Let's go swimming in the _____.

Mr. Frog's Dream

Once upon a time a frog lived in a pond. He jumped higher than any other frog in the pond. He swam faster than any other frog. He sang more sweetly than any other frog. His friends and family called him Mr. Frog.

Mr. Frog spoke day and night about what he did. He told everyone he was a wonderful frog.

Soon no one wanted to listen to Mr. Frog's speeches. The other animals ran away from him. Mr. Frog spoke to the birds who stopped at the pond. They did not have to listen day and night. They listened a short time and flew away.

Winter came. Mr. Frog went to sleep in the mud at the bottom of the pond. Then spring came. Mr. Frog woke up and swam to the top of the water. He did not jump or swim or sing or talk. He sat quietly on a flower on the pond. Sometimes he put out his sticky tongue to catch an insect. The frogs and birds asked, "Why is he so quiet?"

Mr. Frog was thinking about a dream he had that winter. In the dream he was flying to ponds in other countries.

Mr. Frog made a sad sound. Everyone in the pond heard it. Friends and family came to him. They knew something was wrong. They wanted to help him. "Mr. Frog, what is the matter?" asked one of his cousins.

Mr. Frog was happy. Everyone wanted him to speak! He sat up like a king. Mr. Frog said, "I had a wonderful dream. Listen to it!"

The other frogs knew they could not stop him. "Tell us what you dreamed!" they said.

"You will not believe it," said Mr. Frog, looking up at the sky. "I dreamed that I was flying in the sky like a bird. Yes, just like a bird. And now I know how I can do it!"

"Wonderful!" all the frogs said. "Tell us how to do it!"

"No, that is my secret," Mr. Frog said proudly. "No other frog can do what I can. Only I can fly."

Suddenly Mr. Frog heard two wild ducks. "Cua, cua," they said. They came down on the water next to Mr. Frog. They were his friends.

"We are glad to see you again, Mr. Frog," they said. "Did you sleep well this winter?"

"Very well," he answered. "I dreamed that you took me flying in the air. Will you help me make my dream come true?"

The ducks laughed. "How can we do this?"

"I remember how. It was in my dream. We must find a stick. Each of you will take one end of the stick in your mouth. I will hold the center in my mouth. Then we shall fly together! That is just how it was in my dream."

"We can take you over the pond. Maybe we can take you to the field next to the pond," said the ducks.

"Thank you," Mr. Frog answered. He wanted the other animals in the pond to see him flying.

"You must remember one thing," said a duck. "You must not speak when we are flying."

"I know that!" answered Mr. Frog. He felt very proud. "I always know what to do!"

The news passed quickly from one animal to the next. Everyone came to see Mr. Frog fly with the ducks.

The ducks took the stick in their mouths. Mr. Frog held the center of the stick in his mouth. Together they flew above the pond. Everyone watched them.

Mr. Frog was never so happy in his life. He wanted to fly forever.

Mr. Frog thought to himself, "Maybe they will take me with them to other ponds. All the animals will say how wonderful we are!"

Each time the ducks circled the pond, they flew faster and faster. Mr. Frog got dizzy.

"Slow down!" he said.

With those words he let go of the stick. Mr. Frog fell down from the sky. He fell into the pond with a big S-P-L-A-S-H.

The other frogs found Mr. Frog floating sadly in the water.

One of his cousins asked, "What happened?" Mr. Frog did not look at him. He just said, "I don't want to talk about it."
    And he didn't.

Understanding the Story

A. *When Does It Happen?*

Put these sentences in the correct order. Write **1** next to the sentence that tells what happened first.

_____ The ducks flew in a circle with Mr. Frog.

_____ Mr. Frog told the other frogs his dream.

_____ Mr. Frog fell into the pond.

_____ The ducks promised to help Mr. Frog.

_____ Mr. Frog had a dream about flying.

_____ Mr. Frog got dizzy.

_____ The ducks told Mr. Frog not to talk while flying.

_____ Mr. Frog said, "Slow down!"

_____ Mr. Frog didn't want to talk about it.

B. *Telling the Story Again*

Fill in the blanks. Use the words you learned in **Practicing New Words**.

Mr. Frog liked to talk a lot, so the other animals ran away from him. In the winter he slept in the _____ at the bottom of the pond. In the spring he told his friends he dreamed he was flying. Two ducks promised to help him fly. They warned him not to speak while flying. Then they put a stick in their mouths. Mr. Frog held the center of the stick in his mouth. Together they flew around the _____. Mr. Frog got _____. He said, "Slow down!" He fell down when he spoke. The other frogs found him _____ing on top of the water.

C. Looking Back

Answer these questions.
1. Why didn't the animals want to listen to Mr. Frog?
2. What did Mr. Frog do in his dream?
3. Where did the ducks fly with Mr. Frog?
4. Why did Mr. Frog get dizzy?
5. Why didn't Mr. Frog want to talk about what happened?

Exploring the Meaning

A. Making Friends

Complete the chart. Then answer the question.

Character	When	What He/ They Did	What He/ They Said
Mr. Frog	day and night	*talked*	*I am wonderful.*
Mr. Frog	in the winter		*nothing*
Mr. Frog		made a sad sound	
the ducks		took him flying	
Mr. Frog	the day he flew		
the other animals			What happened?

What happens when people talk too much?

B. *Thinking About the Story*

Finish these sentences.

1. When Mr. Frog talked about himself, the other animals

   _____.

2. Mr. Frog asked the ducks to help him because

   _____.

3. They agreed to help, but they told Mr. Frog

   _____.

4. Mr. Frog fell from the sky because

   _____.

C. *In Everyday Life*

Talk about these questions.

1. Why do some people talk a lot?
2. Do you think frogs are funny animals? Guess why the main character in this story is a frog.
3. What should you do to make and keep friends?

The Blue Cat

INDONESIAN

Indonesia is a country in Southeast Asia. It includes more than 13,000 islands! People live on 6,000 of the islands. Most Indonesians are farmers.

Before You Read

Talk about these questions.
1. Why do many people like to have pet cats?
2. Why are cats useful on ships and in towns and cities?
3. Look at the picture for this story. How do you think the king feels about cats? Why?

Practicing New Words

You will find these words in the story. Study their meanings.

collar	a band around the neck of a dog or other pet
cushion	a pillow

dye	a material used to color things
fortune-teller	a person who tells the future
fur	thick hair on an animal
kingdom	land belonging to a king
lap	the top of your legs when you sit
prison	jail
reward	a prize for doing something good
ruby	an expensive red stone used in jewelry
silk	a soft material made from the thread of a silkworm
tub	a large container for washing

Fill in the blanks with the new words. Use each word only once.

1. The woman put a _____ on every hard kitchen chair.

2. Sally got a pair of _____ earrings for her birthday.

3. The dog has long, black _____.

4. The _____ told the king, "Somebody will visit you tomorrow!"

5. The princess wore a purple _____ dress.

6. The police are giving a $5,000 _____ to the person who finds the bank robber.

7. The little boy sat on his grandfather's _____ and listened to his stories.

8. My cat has a _____ on its neck with its name and address written on it.

9. Mother put the baby in the _____ and gave him a bath.

10. Everyone in the _____ knows the king is looking for a blue cat.

11. I want to buy black _____ to color my old brown shoes.

12. The police caught the thief and took him to _____.

The Blue Cat

Once upon a time there was a king in Indonesia. He loved cats. He always had a cat near him. All of his cats were beautiful.

His favorite cat was white. It had a collar made of gold and rubies. It slept on a silk cushion. The king played and talked with his cat.

One morning the king told his fortune-teller, "I dreamed about a blue cat with green-yellow eyes and a ruby collar. It lay on my lap when I sat on my throne. Everyone brought me gifts. Everyone was happy. The blue cat brought me good luck. But when the cat jumped off my lap and ran out of the palace, the gifts disappeared. Tell me what my dream means."

The fortune-teller said, "You had a wonderful dream. A blue cat will bring riches and happiness to everyone on the island. In your dream the cat went away and the happiness went away, too. We must find a blue cat to bring back your good luck."

The fortune-teller was telling the king a story to trick him. But the king was sure he was speaking wise words.

The king told all his people, "Bring me a blue cat."

Everyone looked for a blue cat. There were plenty of white and black cats and gray and orange cats. But no one had a blue cat.

The king promised a large reward for a blue cat. He promised to give his daughter in marriage and half of his kingdom to any young man who found the blue cat of his dreams.

A young man in the country loved the princess. He heard the king's promise. He thought and thought. At last he brought a blue cat to the king.

Some people in the palace said it looked like the king's favorite white cat. It was the same size. It had green-yellow eyes. But it was bright blue. It was the first time anyone saw a blue cat.

The king did not ask questions. The blue cat was wearing a collar of rubies, like the cat in his dream. The king and his

people were happy. The people of the land brought the king gifts. Life was just like his dream.

"I promised to give my daughter in marriage to the finder of the blue cat. This young man will marry the princess and receive half of my kingdom," said the king.

Many people spoke secretly about the blue cat. They said it wasn't a blue cat. They said it was really the white cat. They thought the young man painted its fur blue. People said, "How can this young man trick our king?"

One day the blue cat was gone.

The king thought that bad luck was coming to the palace. He must find the blue cat! The servants looked in all the rooms. They found no blue cat.

Then someone looked in the garden. There was the king's cat. When it ran away, it fell into a tub of soapy water. The strong soap took most of the blue dye off its fur.

The king saw the cat. He was very angry! "My daughter's husband tricked me. Now he must die. Prison is too good for him. My luck depends on a real blue cat."

The princess loved her husband very much. She did not want him to die. "What are you doing, Father?" she cried. "You wanted a blue cat. My husband made you a blue cat. You wanted our land to be happy. This blue cat brought us peace."

"But I wanted the blue cat of my dreams. The fortune-teller said, 'A blue cat will bring you good luck.'" The old king didn't want to listen to the princess's words.

"The blue cat was only a dream, my dear father. My husband showed you that a dream is only a dream. Happiness comes when you believe in the dream. You were happy when you thought the white cat was a blue cat. Your white cat is just like a real blue cat if you think so," cried the princess.

Just then the white cat jumped on the king's lap. It still had a little blue color on its fur. The king thought about his daughter's words. Then he laughed and played with the cat.

"Give the cat another bath," he said. "Wash out the blue dye. My daughter is right. A white cat is just like a blue cat. There will be no more dream cats in my kingdom."

Understanding the Story

A. *What Happens?*

Choose **a, b,** or **c** to complete each sentence.

1. The fortune-teller said the king's dream meant
   a. he must find a white cat.
   b. he must find a blue cat.
   c. he must let the blue cat go free.

2. The king said, "Any man who finds a blue cat
   a. will marry my daughter as a reward."
   b. will get half of my kingdom as a reward."
   c. will get half of my kingdom and marry my daughter."

3. Many people in the kingdom thought the king's blue cat was
   a. really his white cat.
   b. really blue.
   c. really beautiful.

4. The king learned that the blue cat was really white when
   a. the young man told him he put blue dye on the cat.
   b. the blue cat fell into a tub of soapy water.
   c. his daughter washed the blue cat.

5. At the end the king decided to
   a. play with his white cat.
   b. put the young man in prison.
   c. dye his white cat blue again.

B. *Telling the Story Again*

Fill in the blanks. Use the words you learned in **Practicing New Words**.

The king's favorite white cat wore a beautiful _____
and gold _____. It slept on a soft _____
made of _____.

   When the king had a dream, he asked his _____
what the dream meant. The fortune-teller told the king to find a cat
with blue _____.

   The king promised a _____ to the finder of a blue

cat. He promised to give half of his _____ and his daughter in marriage to the finder of a blue cat.

A young man loved the princess. He bought blue _____ to color the king's cat. Then he caught the white cat and colored it blue. The blue cat made the king happy. The young man married the princess. They were happy, too.

One day the cat ran out of the palace. It fell into a _____ of soapy water, so the blue dye came off. The king was angry because the young man tricked him. He wanted to send the young man to _____, but his daughter told him that was not the right thing to do.

The king understood. The cat jumped up on his _____. The king wasn't angry anymore.

C. Looking Back

Answer these questions.

1. Where did the king's favorite cat sleep?
2. What did it wear?
3. What did the king dream?
4. What did the fortune-teller tell the king to do?
5. What did the young man do to the cat?
6. How did the king discover the young man tricked him?
7. Why didn't the king send the young man to prison?

Exploring the Meaning

A. Discovering the Truth

Complete the chart. Then answer the question.

When?	Color of the Cat	Why?	How Did the King Feel?
the beginning of the story	*white*	*It was born that color.*	*He loved the cat.*
the middle of the story			
the end of the story			

What does the king learn about the importance of the color of the cat?

B. *Thinking About the Story*

Finish these sentences.

1. The king dreamed about a blue cat that

   _____.

2. The fortune-teller said they must

   _____.

3. The fortune-teller tricked the king. We all know

   _____.

4. The young man tricked the king when he

   _____.

5. Everyone was happy until the blue cat

   _____.

6. The princess helped her father understand that

   _____.

C. In Everyday Life

Talk about these questions.

1. The young man put dye on the cat's fur. Why do people sometimes put dye on their hair?
2. Do you believe in dreams? Why or why not?
3. How can you make a dream come true?

The Little Orphan

TURKISH

A small part of Turkey is in southeastern Europe. The rest of Turkey is in Asia, so it is a Middle Eastern country. Turkey played a very important part in history. Its kings built the Ottoman Empire. This empire lasted for six hundred years and included countries in Europe, Asia, and North Africa.

Before You Read

Talk about these questions.
1. Find Turkey on a map. Why do you think its location made Turkey an important country in history?
2. When a child's parents die, the child is an orphan. What problems do orphans have?
3. Who takes care of orphans in your country?

Practicing New Words

You will find these words in the story. Study their meanings.

bat	a mouselike animal with wings
chameleon	a reptile that changes colors
handsome	good-looking
jug	a container for liquids with a handle and a place to pour from
lizard	a reptile that looks like a small alligator
orphan	a child with no parents
oxen	plural of *ox*; male cows
(to) pick	to take fruit and vegetables off plants
polite	well-behaved; having good manners
rude	badly behaved; having bad manners
sugarcane	very tall grass used to make sugar
toad	an animal that looks like a frog but does not live in the water

Fill in the blanks with the new words. Use each word only once.

1. The _____ jumped from plant to plant and ate flies.

2. Why is every prince _____? Aren't there any ugly princes?

3. Mother poured lemonade from a _____.

4. The little girl was an _____. Her parents were killed in an automobile accident.

5. _____ is an important agricultural product.

6. A _____ flies at night and has excellent hearing.

7. The _____ pulled the heavy wagon.

8. A _____ will change its color to be like the world around it.

9. Children should be _____ to parents and teachers.

10. You were very _____ when you came into the middle of our conversation.

11. The lemons are yellow, so let's go _____ a few of them.

12. A _____ has short legs and a body like a dinosaur.

The Little Orphan

Once upon a time there were seven brothers. They were all strong and handsome except the youngest one. He was weak and ugly. His brothers laughed at him. Then the boys' parents died. The six brothers made their youngest brother do all the hard and dirty work. His life was very unhappy. So he thought, "I will look for the god Zanahari. I will ask him to help me."

The little orphan got up early one morning. He ran out of the house. On the road, he met an old man. "Where are you going?" asked the man.

"I want to see Zanahari," answered the little orphan. "Can you tell me how to find him?"

"Yes," said the old man. "Cross this mountain. On the other side there is a sugarcane field. It belongs to Zanahari. Do not touch the sugarcane. Keep going and soon you will see Zanahari's sheep. Do not disturb them. Next you will come to Zanahari's orange trees. The oranges are large and beautiful, but do not pick any. Then you will see another mountain. Climb over it and you will see Zanahari's oxen. Don't throw stones at them. After that you will see a beautiful, clear pond. Don't drink from it; it belongs to Zanahari. Finally you will reach Zanahari's house. His wife will answer the door. Be polite to her. She will give you some water. Do not touch the jug when you drink."

The little orphan thanked the old man. He smiled and left.

The boy climbed the mountain and saw a field of juicy sugarcane. He did not touch it. He kept walking and saw some fat sheep. He did not disturb them. Then he came to some orange trees. He was hungry and thirsty. He wanted to eat an orange, but he didn't. He crossed another mountain and found some oxen. He did not disturb them. He came to a beautiful pond. He was very thirsty, but he did not drink.

Finally the orphan reached Zanahari's house. The god's wife answered the door. The boy politely asked her for some water. She brought him a jug. He did not touch it. He opened his mouth and she poured water into his mouth.

Zanahari came into the room and asked, "What is your wish?"

"I want to be strong and handsome."

"When you were on your way here, did you see my sugarcane field?"

"Yes, I did, but I did not touch it."

"Did you see my sheep?"

"Yes, I did, but I did not disturb them."

"And my oranges?"

"I saw them, but I did not pick any."

"Did you see my oxen?"

"Yes, I did, but I did not throw any stones at them."

"And my pond?"

"It was clear, but I did not drink from it."

Zanahari asked his wife, "When you gave him water, did he touch the jug?"

"No, he did not," she answered. "He was very polite."

Zanahari put his hand on the little orphan's head. He made him strong and handsome. The happy orphan thanked Zanahari and went home. His brothers were very surprised.

"What happened to you? Where were you?" they asked.

"You know I was unhappy. I went to see Zanahari. He changed me."

The six brothers thought, "We'll go see him, too. Then Zanahari will make us stronger and more handsome." The brothers went out to the road. There they met the old man. He gave them the same directions he gave their youngest brother. But the six brothers did not follow the directions. "No one will see us," they said.

Finally they reached Zanahari's house. The god asked, "What do you want?"

"We want to be stronger and more handsome."

"Did you see my sugarcane field on the way here?"

"Yes, we did, and we picked some sugarcane."

"Did you see my sheep?"

"Yes. We were hungry, so we ate one."

"Did you see my oranges?"

"Yes, we ate some."

"You didn't throw stones at my oxen, did you?"

"Yes, we did."

"Did you drink from my pond?"

"Yes, we did."

Then Zanahari asked his wife, "Did they behave well?"

"No, they were rude," she said. "They took the water jug in their hands, too."

Zanahari was angry. "You were rude and did not follow the directions. You behaved like animals. I will turn you into animals." He changed them into a lizard, a snake, a frog, a toad, a bat, and a chameleon. They all ran away into the mountains.

The youngest brother got everything that belonged to the family. He lived happily ever after.

Understanding the Story

A. What Happens?

Match the sentence parts. Write the correct letter in each blank.

_____ 1. The six brothers made

    a. to be stronger and more handsome.

_____ 2. The old man told

    b. to Zanahari for help.

_____ 3. The little orphan went

    c. to be strong and handsome.

_____ 4. The little orphan politely asked

    d. their little brother unhappy.

_____ 5. The little orphan wanted

    e. the boy what to do.

_____ 6. The six brothers wanted

    f. Zanahari's wife for water.

B. Telling the Story Again

Fill in the blanks. Use the words you learned in **Practicing New Words**.

The little orphan wanted to be _____ and strong like his brothers. He was an _____, so he had no parents to help him. On his way to Zanahari's house he wanted to eat the sweet _____ in the fields, but he did not _____ it. He did not throw stones at the _____ or eat the oranges or sheep. He asked for water, but he did not touch the _____. He was very _____ to Zanahari's wife. Zanahari made his wish come true.

The other six brothers were different. They threw stones, ate everything they wanted, and did everything the old man said not to do. They were _____ to Zanahari's wife. Because they acted like animals, Zanahari changed them into a _____, a _____, a _____, a chameleon, a frog, and a snake.

C. Looking Back

Answer these questions.

1. Why did the little orphan go to Zanahari for help?
2. How did the little orphan behave on his way to Zanahari's house?
3. What wish came true for the little orphan?
4. How did the six brothers behave on the way to Zanahari's house?
5. What did Zanahari do to them?

Exploring the Meaning

A. Controlling Yourself

Complete the chart. Then answer the question.

What?	Direction	Orphan's Behavior	Brothers' Behavior
sugarcane	*not to touch*	*didn't touch*	*touched*
sheep			
oranges			
oxen			
Zanahari's wife	be polite		

How was the little orphan's behavior different from his brothers' behavior?

B. *Thinking About the Story*

Finish these sentences.

1. The older brothers made the little orphan feel bad because they _____.

2. They did not keep their promise to the old man because they thought _____.

3. The god changed them into animals because they _____.

4. Zanahari made the little orphan's wish come true because he behaved _____.

C. *In Everyday Life*

Talk about these questions.

1. Why do some people act like the six brothers?
2. Why is it difficult to behave like the little orphan?
3. Why is it important to be polite?

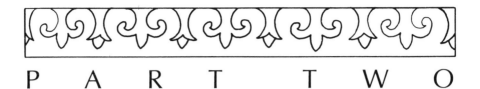

PART TWO

TRYING *to* WIN

Why the Monsoon Comes Each Year

VIETNAMESE

Vietnam is in Southeast Asia. China, France, and Japan each controlled Vietnam at one time in history. Many Vietnamese people are farmers in villages, but about six million people live in Vietnam's two large cities: Hanoi and Ho Chi Minh City.

Before You Read

Talk about the following.

1. Vietnam has monsoons every year between April and October. A *monsoon* is a strong wind that blows from the Indian Ocean and brings a lot of rain. What kinds of weather does your country have every year?

2. Look at the picture for this story. Guess which person is the mountain god. Which is the sea god? What are they doing?

Practicing New Words

You will find these words in the story. Study their meanings.

(to) arrive	to come
diamond	a very expensive, hard stone, usually clear in color
emerald	an expensive, green stone
(to) follow	to go after
pearl	a white material made by oysters inside their shells, often used in jewelry
powerful	very strong
(to) pray	to speak or sing to one's god
trick	something done to fool or cheat someone
wave	water or air moving up and down again and again
wedding	a ceremony for two people to become husband and wife
wrinkle	a line in a person's skin, often a mark of age

Fill in the blanks with the new words. Use each word only once.

1. A strong ocean _____ fell on the beach.
2. Two hundred people came to the _____ of the famous singer and her boyfriend.
3. I found this _____ in an oyster shell.
4. A _____ looks like glass, but it is very expensive.
5. Do you see a _____ on my face?
6. I hope you didn't use a _____ to win the game.
7. Alexander the Great was a _____ emperor and ruler.
8. When will your airplane _____ in New York?
9. I want an _____ necklace because green is my favorite color.
10. The people will _____ for rain because it is so dry.
11. Did that dog _____ you home from school?

Why the Monsoon Comes
Each Year

Princess Mi Nuong was sad. A servant combed her shiny black hair and helped her with her beautiful dress. The servant held up a mirror, but Mi Nuong pushed it away. The princess didn't want to see the small new wrinkle between her eyes. She was getting old, and she didn't have a husband.

Many men wanted to marry the princess. Some were handsome. Many came from other lands. But the emperor did not want his daughter to marry any of them. He wanted her to marry someone rich and powerful. Many years passed, and the princess thought she would never marry.

One day two strangers came to the emperor. Both were rich and powerful. One was the sea god. The other was the mountain god. The emperor told them to come the next day with wedding gifts. The one that arrived first would marry the princess.

The sea god hurried to his men. He told them to look for perfect pearls and delicious sea food. The mountain god climbed to the highest mountain. He told his men to find diamonds and emeralds. He also told them to fill baskets with special fruits that did not grow in the emperor's land.

The men quickly found the diamonds, emeralds, and fruit. The mountain god hurried down the mountain with the gifts. He arrived at the palace very early in the morning. The emperor was happy with the gifts. Mi Nuong and the mountain god married. The emperor promised to visit his daughter in her new home.

A few minutes later the sea god arrived with his gifts. He saw Mi Nuong leaving the palace with the mountain god. He was very angry. He thought the mountain god used some trick to arrive first.

The sea god told his men to follow the mountain god and take Mi Nuong from him. A strong wind began to blow. Rain

fell, and the sea waves got higher and higher. Water came on the land. People had to run away from the sea and the rivers. The water washed away houses and large cities.

The water went up to the foot of the mountain. But the sea god could not catch Mi Nuong. The mountain god told his men to throw trees and big rocks down on the sea god and his men.

They fought for many days. The people prayed for them to stop. Many people died in the high water.

Finally the sea god stopped fighting. He could not take the princess from the mountain god. He and his men went back to the sea. He took the high water with him.

But the sea god didn't stop being angry. Every year he tries to take the princess from the mountain god. He sends strong winds and high water onto the land. Every year he comes to the mountain where Mi Nuong lives with her husband. The mountain god pushes him back into the sea. That is why the monsoon comes to Vietnam every year.

Understanding the Story

A. When Does It Happen?

Put these sentences in the correct order. Write **1** next to the sentence that tells what happened first.

_____ The sea god stopped fighting.

_____ The mountain god married the princess.

_____ The sea god got angry.

_____ The sea god and the mountain god looked for gifts.

_____ The sea god followed the princess with rain and wind.

_____ The sea god and the mountain god both wanted to marry the princess.

_____ The sea god arrived with his gifts.

_____ The mountain god arrived with his gifts.

_____ The sea god and the mountain god fought for many days.

_____ The sea god went back to the sea.

B. Telling the Story Again

Fill in the blanks. Use the words you learned in **Practicing New Words**.

Princess Mi Nuong was sad. She had a new _____
on her face. She was getting older and had no husband.

   One day two strangers came: the mountain god and the sea
god. Both men wanted to marry her. Her father, the emperor, told
them to bring _____ gifts. The sea god went to find
perfect _____s and delicious sea food. The mountain
god looked for _____s and green _____s.

   The mountain god _____d first. He married Mi
Nuong and they left. The sea god came too late. He told his men
to _____ the princess with wind and rain. One
_____ after another hit the mountain. It was the first
monsoon. But the sea god did not catch Mi Nuong. The people
_____ed for the monsoon to stop. Many people died.
Then it stopped.

C. Looking Back

Answer these questions.

1. Why didn't the princess marry when she was young?

2. What kind of man did her father want her to marry?

3. What gifts did the mountain god tell his men to find?

4. What gifts did the sea god tell his men to find?

5. What did the sea god do to show he was angry?

6. What is the purpose of this story?

Exploring the Meaning

A. Who Marries the Princess?

Complete the chart. Then answer the question.

What Happened?	Sea God	Mountain God
When did he arrive?	*second*	
What gifts did he bring?	*pearls and sea food*	
Did he marry the princess?	*no*	
How did he show power?	*strong winds and rain*	

How did the emperor choose Mi Nuong's husband?

B. Thinking About the Story

Finish these sentences.

1. The princess was sad because

   _____.

2. She was not married because

   _____.

3. The mountain god and the sea god wanted

   _____.

4. The emperor told them to

   _____.

5. The princess married the mountain god because
   _____.

6. The story says that monsoons come every year to Vietnam
   because _____.

C. *In Everyday Life*

Talk about these questions.

1. What other stories do you know that explain happenings in nature?
2. Why do people tell stories to explain happenings in nature?
3. Think of a time you didn't get something you wanted very much. Tell what happened.

The Tortoise Wins a Race

BRAZILIAN

Brazil is the largest country in South America in population and in size. It has the world's largest tropical rain forest and many large, modern cities. The main language of Brazil is Portuguese.

Before You Read

Talk about these questions.

1. Look at a map of South America. What great river is in Brazil?

2. What kinds of animals live in Brazil's tropical rain forest?

3. Look at the picture for this story. What kinds of animals do you see?

Practicing New Words

You will find these words in the story. Study their meanings.

clearing an open place in a jungle or forest

deer a thin, fast animal that lives in the jungle or forest; a mammal

edge side of

flute a long, thin musical instrument with a hole to blow into

jaguar a large, spotted jungle cat

meeting a planned gathering

relatives members of a family

scared frightened; afraid

tortoise a large turtle that moves very slowly

vine a plant that needs something to climb on

Fill in the blanks with the new words. Use each word only once.

1. The _____ attacked the zebra and killed it.

2. How many _____ are coming to the wedding?

3. Are you _____ of snakes?

4. The little girl played a _____ in the concert.

5. A _____ can live for 500 years, maybe because it moves so slowly!

6. Grapes grow on a _____.

7. The animals came to the _____ in the jungle.

8. The _____ ran away quickly from the lion.

9. The farmer built a house at the _____ of the forest.

10. I have a _____ at 10:00, so I cannot talk to you.

The Tortoise Wins a Race

A tortoise named Jabotí lived in the Amazon jungle. He played a flute. All the other animals wanted his instrument, but he never gave it to anybody.

One day Jabotí was walking and playing his flute. He saw Suasú, the deer.

"Hello, Jabotí," said the deer. "Where are you going?"

"Good morning," said Jabotí. "I'm going to visit my cousin."

"Where did you get that flute?" asked the deer.

"I killed a jaguar and made the flute from his bone."

"You killed a jaguar? I don't believe it!" said the deer. "You couldn't kill a fly. Everyone in the jungle knows that!"

"You think that I am weak. You are wrong," said Jabotí. "Tell me something. What can you do best of all?"

"I can run," answered Suasú.

"All right. Then let's have a race!" said Jabotí.

Suasú laughed and laughed. "Do you really think you can race with me?" she asked.

"I can race with you," said Jabotí.

"Okay, let's begin right now," said the deer.

"I'm busy today," said Jabotí. "We can race tomorrow. You can run in this clearing. I know you can't run in the jungle. It is full of vines. I'll run near the edge of the jungle. When you want to know where I am, just call out and I'll answer you. Okay?"

"That is fair," answered the deer. "I have an idea, too. The winner of the race gets your flute."

Jabotí was scared. What if he lost his flute? But he couldn't say no now.

"Okay," said Jabotí. He sounded brave, but he was scared.

That night Jabotí asked his family and friends to come to a meeting.

"Friends and relatives, this is a very important meeting,"

said Jabotí. "Tomorrow I am running a race with Suasú, the deer. I must win this race."

"That's foolish!" shouted the tortoises. "Jabotí is crazy. He can't run a race with a deer! We must do something, or he will get all of us in trouble!"

Jabotí said, "Just a minute, everybody. Let me finish." He quietly told them his plan. They all listened.

The next day Suasú came to the clearing. She was surprised to hear Jabotí's voice in the jungle.

"Good morning, my friend Suasú. Here I am, ready to go. Are you ready?"

"Ready," answered the deer.

"One . . . two . . . three . . . go!" shouted the tortoise.

Suasú thought that she would win the race easily. She walked a little way. Then she looked back and called, "Jabotí!" The answer came from the jungle—ahead of her!

"Here I am. You must hurry or I will win!"

The deer was very surprised. "How did he get ahead of me?" she asked herself. Suasú began to run.

A little later she called again. Again a voice answered from ahead of her: "Here I am, Suasú."

Suasú ran faster. But when she called again, she heard a voice in the jungle ahead of her: "Here I am, Suasú."

So the race continued. The deer ran as fast as she could. The tortoise's voice always came from the jungle ahead of her. Finally Suasú couldn't run anymore. She was too tired.

Jabotí found her lying on the ground. Her tongue was hanging out.

"Well," said Jabotí. "A tortoise *can* win a race against a deer! You thought that you could get my flute. But look at you! You are too tired to move."

Jabotí was very happy. His plan worked. His friends and family helped him. Each tortoise took a place in the jungle, near the clearing. When Suasú called Jabotí, the tortoise ahead of her answered.

Jabotí took his flute and went away. He walked and played a happy song for everyone to hear.

Understanding the Story

A. *What Happens?*

Choose **a, b,** or **c** to complete each sentence.

1. Jabotí wanted to race later because
    a. he was too busy to run immediately.
    b. he needed time to practice for the race.
    c. he needed time to tell his friends and relatives about his plan.

2. Suasú wanted to race with Jabotí because
    a. she thought she could win the flute.
    b. she wanted to prove she could run faster.
    c. he killed a jaguar.

3. Jabotí's relatives and friends helped him in the race because
    a. they felt sorry for him.
    b. they thought he was foolish.
    c. they thought they would all get in trouble if he lost.

4. Jabotí won the race because
    a. his friends and relatives helped him.
    b. he really ran faster than the deer.
    c. the deer went to sleep in the middle of the race.

B. *Telling the Story Again*

Fill in the blanks. Use the words you learned in **Practicing New Words**.

Jabotí knew that all the animals in the jungle wanted his wonderful
_____. One day he met Suasú the _____
in the jungle. He said he made the flute out of the bone of a
_____. Jabotí made a bet with the deer to race, but
he felt _____ because he knew he could not run at
all. Suasú laughed when the _____ said he wanted
to race with her.

That night Jabotí called a _____ of his friends and
_____. They listened to his plan. They agreed to help
Jabotí.

The next day the deer ran in the _____ in the jungle

so she would not fall on a _____ growing between the trees. The tortoise "ran" near the _____ of the jungle.

Jabotí won because his friends and relatives each took one part of the way. They did not have to run at all!

C. Looking Back

Answer these questions.

1. What did Jabotí have that the other animals wanted?
2. Why did Suasú laugh when Jabotí said he wanted to race with her?
3. Why did Suasú race with Jabotí?
4. Why did Jabotí win the race?

Exploring the Meaning

A. Comparing Two Animals

Complete the chart. Then answer the questions.

Describing the Animal	Deer	Tortoise
kind of animal	*mammal*	*reptile*
how it protects itself		
how it moves		
where it lives		

How are a deer and a tortoise alike? How are they different? Do you think a tortoise could really win a race against a deer? Why or why not?

B. Thinking About the Story

Finish these sentences.

1. The tortoise got himself into trouble when he told the deer that _____.

2. We know that Suasú was very tired at the end of the race because _____.

3. The tortoise did not really win the race by running. He won it by _____.

C. In Everyday Life

Talk about these questions.

1. *Cooperation* means working together to get a job done. What message does this story give us about cooperation?

2. Jabotí wins the race dishonestly. Suasú runs an honest race. How does this story make you feel? Are all winners dishonest?

3. Suasú has good muscles, but Jabotí can think through his problem and find an answer. Why is it sometimes more important to use your head instead of your muscles? What other examples can you think of?

4. How can this story help you in the future?

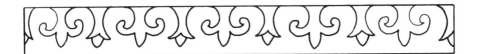

The Lazy Fox

ARGENTINEAN

Argentina covers most of southern South America. Spain controlled this country for more than three hundred years. People came from many European countries to live in Argentina. Only a small number of Native Americans live in Argentina today. The main language of Argentina is Spanish.

Before You Read

Talk about the following.

1. What do you know about foxes? Do you know any sayings about foxes?

2. Look at the picture for this story. Guess why the fox is talking to the armadillo. What are the armadillos eating?

Practicing New Words

You will find these words in the story. Study their meanings.

armadillo	a tropical mammal with bony plates (see picture)
armor	a hard covering to protect the body
(to) crack	to break; to split into pieces
crop	any plant a farmer grows
fox	a small, wild animal of the dog family, with a bushy tail (see picture)
lazy	not liking to work
rock	a stone
root	the bottom part of a plant; the part in the ground
stupid	not intelligent; not smart
tricky	good at cheating or fooling others; full of tricks
wheat	a plant used to make flour

Fill in the blanks with the new words. Use each word only once.

1. Rice is a very important _____ in Asia.
2. _____ people do not want to work.
3. A _____ got into the chicken house and ate a chicken.
4. Don't drop that plate or it will _____!
5. A carrot is the _____ of that plant.
6. An _____ is an animal with armor.
7. The storm made a large _____ fall down the mountain.
8. It's _____ to go to a party the night before a test. You should study and get some sleep instead.
9. Be careful when you talk to that man. He's very _____.
10. Most bread is made from _____.
11. Long ago, soldiers wore _____ to protect themselves.

The Lazy Fox

A tricky fox had a farm. He was too lazy to work on his farm. No one wanted to work for him.

One morning he said, "I must plant something in my fields, or I will be hungry. What can I do?" He thought and thought. Finally he had an idea.

"I will tell my neighbor, a stupid armadillo, to plant my fields. I will promise to give him a part of the crop. But it will only be a very small part."

The fox went to see the armadillo. "Good day, my friend," the fox called. "I want to help you."

"Help me?" asked the armadillo. He could not believe his ears.

"Yes. The land on your farm is dry and full of rocks. Why don't you plant on my good land? As payment, you can give me a small part of your crop."

"You are very kind," answered the armadillo.

The armadillo knew the fox was very smart. He thought the fox had some trick.

"You may plant anything you want," said the fox. "I will take only half of it."

"That is fair," the armadillo said slowly.

"I have a better idea," said the fox. "I will take only the part that grows under the ground. You may have everything that grows above the ground."

"Okay," said the armadillo.

The next morning the armadillo and his family went to the fox's fields. The fox saw them working hard. He was happy with his trick. He did not ask what they were planting.

The plants grew in the rain and the sunshine. Finally it was time to pick the crop.

The armadillo and his family picked a big crop of wheat. But the lazy fox got only roots. The fox was very angry and very hungry. He went to the armadillo's house.

"You made a terrible mistake," the fox shouted at his neighbor. "I cannot eat these roots! You know the good part of the wheat grows above the ground. Next year we will work together again. You take the part that grows under the ground. I will take the part that grows above the ground."

"That is fair," said the armadillo. "Do you want to choose the crop?"

"No, but you must choose it carefully. Just tell me when the food is ready to eat."

The next year the armadillo planted potatoes. Again the crop was very good. The fox got only the tops of the potato plants. The potatoes grew under the ground.

The fox went to his neighbor's farm. "Last year I thought you made a stupid mistake. Now I think you are tricking me. I cannot eat the tops of the potato plants. You never think about me when you plant your crop. See how thin and weak I am."

"You are thin," said the armadillo, "but you look better that way."

The fox was angry. "Next year I will take the tops of the plants and the part that grows under the ground. You take the part that grows in the middle. I must have the bigger part next year. I had nothing for two years."

The armadillo answered, "That is fair."

The fox was happy. He was sure the armadillo could not trick him again.

The next year the armadillo planted corn. The crop was large, with beautiful fat ears of corn in the middle of the plants. The fox got only the roots and the leaves.

The fox ran to the armadillo's house. He and his family were eating some corn. "Come, eat some corn with us," said the armadillo. "Then we can talk about next year's crop."

"No!" said the fox. "You tricked me for three years."

The armadillo said, "I'm sorry. You asked for a part of the crop. I gave you the part you wanted."

The hungry fox looked at the corn. He looked at the armadillo and said to himself, "Why did I call him stupid?"

"Next year I will plant my own crop," said the fox, "and keep all of it!" He went home sadly.

The armadillo took one more ear of corn. He laughed so hard his armor almost cracked.

Understanding the Story

A. What Happens?

Match the sentence parts. Write the correct letter in each blank.

_____ 1. The armadillo planted   a. to get food without doing anything.

_____ 2. The fox told the armadillo   b. hungry each year.

_____ 3. The armadillo laughed   c. he could plant a crop in his field.

_____ 4. The fox was   d. the parts of plants he couldn't eat.

_____ 5. The armadillo was   e. potatoes the second year.

_____ 6. The lazy fox got   f. and almost cracked his armor.

_____ 7. The lazy fox tried   g. hardworking and smart.

B. Telling the Story Again

Fill in the blanks. Use the words you learned in **Practicing New Words**.

The _____ didn't like to work, but he was hungry. He decided to speak to the _____. He thought the armadillo was _____, so he could trick him easily.

He told the armadillo, "My land is good, but yours has _____s everywhere. Why don't you plant your food on my land and give me the part that is underground?" The armadillo was smart. He planted _____ and gave the _____s to the fox. Of course the fox was angry.

The second year the _____ fox told the armadillo he could plant again. This time the armadillo could keep the roots and give the fox everything else. The _____ armadillo planted potatoes and gave the tops to the fox. The fox got angry again.

The third year the fox said the armadillo could keep only the part of the _____ in the middle. The armadillo tricked the fox a third time. He planted corn. The fox was very angry. The armadillo laughed so much that the _____ on his body almost _____ed.

C. Looking Back

Answer these questions.

1. Why did the fox look for the armadillo?
2. What did the armadillo plant each year?
3. Why did the fox get angry each year?
4. Why didn't the fox get anything to eat?

Exploring the Meaning

A. Knowing What to Ask For

Complete the chart. Then answer the question.

Year	Fox Wanted	Armadillo Planted	Fox Got	Armadillo Got
first	*part underground*	*wheat*	*roots*	*wheat*
second				
third				

Why was it so easy for the armadillo to trick the fox?

B. *Thinking About the Story*

Finish these sentences.

1. The fox wanted to trick the armadillo, but instead the armadillo _____.
2. The fox thought the armadillo was stupid, but the armadillo was _____.
3. At the end of the story, the fox was still hungry because _____.
4. The armadillo and his family worked hard, but they always had _____.

C. *In Everyday Life*

Talk about the following.

1. Give examples of how dishonest people can trick or fool honest people.
2. How can you stop others from tricking you?

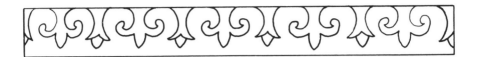

The Giant Bird

NIGERIAN

Nigeria is in western Africa. It has more people than any other country in Africa. This tale is told by the Yoruba, a large tribe in southwestern Nigeria.

Before You Read

Talk about the following.
1. Look at the picture for this story. What do you see?
2. Guess why the giant bird is flying over the village.

Practicing New Words

You will find these words in the story. Study their meanings.

arrow	a sharp stick shot by a bow
(to) attack	to begin a fight

boot	a high shoe, covering the foot and part of the leg
bow	a thin, soft piece of wood used with string to shoot arrows
breast	the front or chest of an animal
claw	the long, sharp nail of a bird or other animal
(to) grab	to take quickly
hunter	a person who looks for animals to kill
(to) lock	to close so a person can only enter with a key
reward	a prize for doing something good
(to) tear	to pull into pieces (past participle: **torn**)
wing	the feathered "arm" of a bird, used to fly

Fill in the blanks with the new words. Use each word only once.

1. The hunter used a _____ and _____ to kill the deer.
2. _____ the door when you leave the house.
3. The _____ of a chicken or turkey is the light-colored meat.
4. Which side _____ed the other in that war?
5. A _____ caught a bear in the forest.
6. Did you _____ your pants when you fell?
7. The bird put its _____s on the branch of the tree.
8. The little bird has a broken _____, so it can't fly.
9. The cowboy wore a _____ on each foot.
10. The woman gave me a _____ for finding her purse.
11. It's late, so I'll _____ some food and return to work.

The Giant Bird

Once upon a time there was a boy named Oni. He was born wearing a pair of boots. When he grew, the boots grew larger, too. He was special in another way. Nothing could kill him. People were afraid of him. They said, "You must leave our village."

Oni went from place to place for a long time. One evening he came to a town. Many bells were ringing. People were hurrying.

Oni met an old man. He said, "My name is Oni. I am a stranger in your town. I have nowhere to go tonight. Will you take me to your house?"

"Yes, come quickly. The bells are ringing, and it is getting dark," answered the old man.

"Why do your people ring bells when it gets dark?" asked Oni.

"Hurry up. We must go inside. Then I will explain the bells," said the man.

They went inside and locked the door. "Now," said the old man, "I will explain. A giant bird comes here every night when it gets dark. We call him Anodo. He stays in our town all night. Anodo kills anyone who is outside. No one knows where this terrible bird comes from. The bells tell the people to go home and lock their doors."

In a few minutes Oni heard the sound of great wings flying over the house. The wings sounded like a big wind. The giant bird flew back and forth over the town. Oni heard the sound of Anodo's wings all night.

In the morning the bird flew away. Oni thanked the old man. Then he went to talk to the king of the town.

"My name is Oni. I have special powers. I want to kill the bird," said Oni.

"I will give half my kingdom to the person who kills Anodo," said the king.

"I will try tonight," said Oni.

Oni returned to the old man's house. He got his bow and arrows and knives.

Evening came. The bells rang. The people ran inside and locked their doors. Oni waited quietly. Soon he heard Anodo's giant wings above the house. All the people of the town were very frightened. Oni was not frightened. He went outside to fight the bird.

Anodo flew down and grabbed Oni with his claws. He flew up into the sky. Oni cut the giant bird's breast with his knife. The bird dropped him. Oni fell to the ground. The giant bird flew down again. Oni shot an arrow into Anodo. The bird threw him to the ground and attacked him with his beak. Oni cut the bird many times with his sharp knife. Anodo attacked Oni again and again. They fought until Oni shot one last arrow at the bird. Anodo fell into a tree. The tree and the dead bird fell on top of Oni.

Oni lay under Anodo's giant wing and the branches of the tree. He slowly got up. One of his boots came off. It was stuck under the dead bird. Oni walked slowly to the river. Then he stopped to sleep.

The next morning the people saw the dead bird. The king asked, "Who killed Anodo?"

A hunter said, "I killed the bird."

"Then you will get the reward. Half my kingdom is yours!" said the king.

People were singing and dancing everywhere. The king invited the hunter to his palace.

Later Oni came to town. He was hurt, and his clothes were torn. He had only one boot. He said to the king, "I killed Anodo! Send someone to look under the bird. He will find my boot there!"

The king told his men to go look under the bird. They returned with the boot. "We found it under the dead bird's wing," they told the king.

"Do you believe me now?" asked Oni. "Ask everyone to try on the boot. Does it fit anyone's foot?"

The boot did not fit anyone. Then Oni said, "Boot from heaven, go on my foot!" The boot moved to Oni and went on his foot. Then everyone believed Oni. The king gave Oni his reward. That night the bells did not ring. The streets were full of dancing people.

Understanding the Story

A. *When Does It Happen?*

Put these sentences in the correct order. Write **1** next to the sentence that tells what happened first.

_____ The boot went on Oni's foot.

_____ Oni and Anodo fought.

_____ Oni listened to the giant bird flying over the town.

_____ Oni went to the town to get his reward.

_____ Oni talked to the king of the town.

_____ Oni heard the bells ringing in the town.

_____ Anodo fell down dead.

_____ Oni had to leave his village.

B. *Telling the Story Again*

Fill in the blanks. Use the words you learned in **Practicing New Words**.

Oni went to a village and heard about a giant bird that came to _____ every night. People had to _____ their doors to keep the bird out of their houses.

Oni decided to kill this terrible bird. He brought his _____ and _____s to shoot the bird. Anodo flew down to _____ Oni with his _____s. But Oni shot the bird in its _____ with his bow and arrow. Finally the bird fell down dead on top of Oni. Oni came out from under Anodo's giant _____, but his _____ was stuck under the bird.

A _____ told the king that he killed Anodo. Then Oni came in his _____ clothes. The king did not believe that he killed Anodo. But Oni told him about the boot under the bird. The king's men found the boot. The king gave half his kingdom to Oni as a _____. The people in the village were happy.

C. Looking Back

Answer these questions.

1. Why did Oni have to leave his village?
2. Why did Oni hear bells ringing in the town?
3. What did Oni decide to do to help that town?
4. Why was it difficult to kill Anodo?
5. What happened when Oni returned to the town?
6. Why did the king later believe Oni?

Exploring the Meaning

A. Facing Problems

Complete the chart. Then answer the question.

Oni's Problem	Why?	What He Did
with his village	*strange boots and power*	
	it wanted to kill him	
with the king		showed his boot

What makes Oni a hero?

B. Thinking About the Story

Finish these sentences.

1. Oni left his village because

   _____.

2. The people in the town rang bells to

   _____.

3. When the giant bird saw Oni, it

   _____.

4. Before Oni returned to the town, a hunter

   _____.

5. The king believed Oni when he

   _____.

C. In Everyday Life

Talk about these questions.

1. In your country, what usually happens to someone who is different from birth?
2. What is a hero?
3. How could a hero make life in your country better?

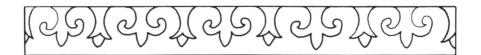

The Man Who Lived a Thousand Years

KOREAN

Korea is in eastern Asia. Until the end of World War II, Korea was one country. In 1945 it became two countries: North Korea and South Korea.

Before You Read

Talk about these questions.
1. Do you think a person can live a thousand years?
2. Why do people live longer today than they did one hundred years ago?
3. Many people want to live a long time. Do you? Why or why not?

Practicing New Words

You will find these words in the story. Study their meanings.

branch	an arm of a tree
brave	not afraid
charcoal	black, partly burned wood often used to make a fire
charm	something that keeps a person safe from danger
foxtail grass	a plant with brushlike spikes
heaven	a world in the sky; a place some people believe they will go after death
judge	a person who decides what is good or correct
messenger	a person sent by someone else to do a job
(to) protect	to keep safe from danger
spirit	the mind and soul of a person; a being with no body
stuck together	joined; not separate
thorn tree	a tree with many short, sharp points

Fill in the blanks with the new words. Use each word only once.

1. The two pieces of paper were _____.
2. _____ looks like the tail of a fox.
3. Can you reach that tree _____ with lemons on it?
4. The _____ fire fighter took the baby out of the burning house.
5. The boy wore a _____ to keep him safe from "the evil eye."
6. Let's buy a bag of _____ to cook the food on our picnic.
7. The plastic will _____ the pictures from the air.
8. Do you think a person's _____ lives forever?
9. He knows a lot about dogs, so he works as a _____ in dog shows.
10. Many people believe that good people go to _____ when they die.
11. The _____ came with an important letter.
12. It's hot! Let's sit under the _____.

The Man Who Lived a Thousand Years

Tong Pang Suk lived for one thousand years. He lived so long because someone in the heavenly kingdom made a mistake. The Book of Life in the heavenly kingdom has every person's name. It tells when each person will come to heaven.

Maybe the pages in the book were stuck together. No one saw Tong Pang Suk's name. No messenger came to take his spirit away from the earth.

Tong lived as long as men usually live. His friends all died, but no one came to take him away. He grew older and older. He lived for hundreds of years.

His friends in the heavenly kingdom asked, "Where is Tong Pang Suk? Why does he stay so long on earth?"

Tong Pang Suk was six hundred years old. He was happy to be alive. He spent most of his time fishing quietly in a river. Tong did not want to die. He was afraid the heavenly messenger was coming to catch him. Every sixty years he took a new name and went to live in a new village. But no messenger found him. He continued to fish.

One day the judges in the heavenly kingdom found Tong's name in the Book of Life. A messenger went to find Tong. The messenger was a spirit, but he looked like a man. He looked all over the earth for Tong Pang Suk. Where was he?

Hundreds of years passed. Then the heavenly messenger heard about a very old man who always fished in the river. He thought, "Maybe the old man is Tong Pang Suk. I have a plan to find out. I'll throw many bags of charcoal into the river near the place where he fishes." He threw the charcoal into the water.

"Why did you do that?" old Tong asked.

"I'm washing my charcoal. Soon it will be white," the messenger answered.

Tong said, "I am nine hundred years old. I never met a foolish man like you. You cannot wash black charcoal and make it white."

The messenger was happy. He found the man he was looking for! He followed Tong everywhere he went. He waited for a chance to take Tong to the heavenly kingdom.

The old man understood that this was the heavenly messenger. "You are brave to follow me," he said to the spirit one day. "These country roads are very dangerous. Aren't you afraid?"

"No, I am not. I am afraid of only four things on this earth," said the spirit. He was not very smart.

"What are you afraid of?" asked Tong.

"A branch from a thorn tree, the shoe of an ox, foxtail grass, and a salt bag. I cannot go to a place where these four things are together. And you, sir," the spirit asked, "what are you afraid of?"

Tong was old, but he was very smart. He said, "I am afraid of roast baby pig and beer."

That day Tong found some foxtail grass, an ox shoe, and an old salt bag. He took them and sat under a thorn tree. He broke a branch off the tree and tied the four things into a charm. The heavenly messenger stood far from the tree. He begged the old man to move away from the tree and leave the charm behind. Tong did not move.

Then the spirit remembered what Tong said. He ran to the village to get some roast baby pig and beer. He threw them at Tong. He wanted to make the old man run away from his charm. But Tong quickly took the roast pig and beer. He ate a delicious meal under the thorn tree with the charm near him.

After that day, Tong Pang Suk carried the charm everywhere he went. The heavenly messenger watched Tong for a hundred years. He waited for the old man to forget his charm.

One day Tong left home without his charm. The messenger took Tong up into the sky.

Since that time the people of Korea put a charm like Tong's on their gates. They make a new one each year. They want their charms to keep away the heavenly messenger so they can live long lives. The charms protect people from many bad spirits. They do not keep people from going to heaven when their time comes.

Understanding the Story

A. What Happens?

Choose **a, b,** or **c** to complete each sentence.

1. Tong
   a. was sad to live so long because all his friends were dead.
   b. was happy to be alive even if his friends and family were dead.
   c. didn't care if he lived or died.

2. The heavenly messenger
   a. couldn't find Tong because he changed his name and address every sixty years.
   b. found Tong easily.
   c. didn't try to find Tong.

3. The heavenly messenger threw charcoal into the river
   a. because he wanted to wash it.
   b. because he didn't want it anymore.
   c. because he wanted Tong to ask about it.

4. The heavenly messenger finally caught Tong
   a. when Tong said he was afraid of roast pig and beer.
   b. when Tong took the roast pig and beer.
   c. when Tong forgot to take his charm with him.

B. *Telling the Story Again*

Fill in the blanks. Use the words you learned in **Practicing New Words**.

Tong Pang Suk was very old. He did not die because nobody found his name in the Book of Life. Maybe the page with his name was _____ with another page. No _____ came to take him up to _____.

One day a _____ in the heavenly kingdom found Tong's name. He sent a messenger to look for Tong.

The messenger saw Tong fishing. He threw some _____ into the river to make Tong talk. When Tong said he was nine hundred years old, the messenger knew it was Tong. Tong told the heavenly messenger he was very _____ to follow him on all the dangerous roads.

Tong made a _____ to keep himself safe. He used four things the messenger was afraid of: the _____ of a _____, the shoe of an ox, _____, and a salt bag. The charm _____ed him from the heavenly messenger. But one day Tong forgot his charm. The messenger took him to heaven.

C. *Looking Back*

Answer these questions.
1. Why didn't Tong die after 70 or 80 years?
2. What did Tong say about the charcoal?
3. What mistake did the messenger make when he talked with Tong?
4. Why did Tong tell the messenger he was afraid of roast pig and beer?
5. Why did Tong die?

Exploring the Meaning

A. *Keeping Death Away*

Complete the chart. Then answer the question.

	Tong	**Messenger**
What did he want to do?	*live*	
What did he say he was afraid of?		
Was he afraid of that?		
Was he very smart?		
Did he get what he wanted? When?	*yes, for 1000 years*	

Why did it take the messenger so long to catch Tong?

B. Thinking About the Story

Finish these sentences.

1. Tong lived a thousand years because

_____.

2. He didn't want the messenger to find him because

_____.

3. The messenger had a problem catching Tong because

_____.

4. The messenger finally caught Tong when

_____.

C. In Everyday Life

Talk about these questions.

1. How can people help themselves live longer?
2. Are you afraid to die? Why or why not?

John Henry

AMERICAN

The United States of America is home to people from all over the world. English is the main language of the United States. This story is about John Henry, an American folk hero. He was a real African-American railroad worker in the 1870s. He tried to stop machines from taking away work from people.

Before You Read

Talk about these questions.
1. Look at the picture of John Henry. Describe this famous man.
2. Did you ever hear "The Ballad of John Henry," a famous American folk song?
3. Why was it difficult to build railroads across the United States? A map of the United States will help you guess the answer.

Practicing New Words

You will find these words in the story. Study their meanings.

(to) beat	to do better than someone else
bet	a promise to give something when someone is right and you are wrong
(to) breathe	to bring air into the body
(to) bury	to put the dead in the ground or sea
dynamite	a strong explosive
hammer	a metal tool used to hit things
hero	a person who does brave things
railroad track	a train rides on this
slave	a person owned by another person
steam drill	a hot-air machine that can make holes in hard materials
steel bar	a long piece of grey metal
tunnel	a way to pass through a mountain or the ground

Fill in the blanks with the new words. Use each word only once.

1. The construction company used _____ to explode the old bridge.
2. John Henry picked up the _____ and hit the big rock.
3. The teenager was a _____ because he saved the lives of many people.
4. He won the _____ and got one hundred dollars.
5. Cars can go through a _____ in the mountain.
6. It is difficult to run away from jail because there are _____s on the windows.
7. I worked fast and I _____ you!
8. Before the Civil War, many people in the southern United States owned _____s.
9. It is sometimes hard to _____ if you run too long.

10. The worker used a _____ to break up the
    sidewalk.

11. The sad family went to the cemetery
    to _____ the young boy.

12. The train rode quickly down the _____.

John Henry

The American Civil War ended. The slaves were free. The United States started at the Atlantic Ocean and ended at the Pacific Ocean. The American people were building farms, houses, factories, bridges, and railroads.

Building railroad tracks was very hard work. Strong men worked on those railroads. John Henry was the most famous railroad worker.

Some people say John Henry was born in Mississippi. Other people say he was born in Tennessee. He grew eight feet tall. John Henry's skin was the color of night. His eyes were like bright stars. He was a very strong man. John Henry was a steel worker for the railroad. He worked hard every day.

The steel workers were the biggest, strongest workers in the world. They pushed long steel bars into the mountains with their hammers. Then they took the bars out of the holes and put in dynamite. When the dynamite exploded, it made tunnels in the mountains.

John Henry was the strongest steel worker in the company. One day a salesman came to town. He showed a new machine to John Henry's boss. It was a steam drill. The salesman said, "This steam drill can make holes in a mountain faster than a man can."

John Henry's boss told the salesman, "I have a steel worker named John Henry. He can drill holes faster than four men working together. My man can beat your drill."

The salesman answered, "I'll make a bet. No man can beat a machine. If your man beats my drill, you can have the drill for free! If he cannot do it, you must buy two drills from me. Is that fair?"

The boss went to see John Henry. "A man here says his steam drill can beat you. Is that true?"

"No, it's not true," said John Henry. "I'll show you. I won't

let that steam drill beat me. I'll die with a hammer in my hand.''

Polly Ann, John Henry's wife, heard the conversation. John Henry called her Pretty Polly. She said to John Henry, "Please don't try."

John Henry laughed and said, "I'm a strong steel worker. Maybe it will kill me, but I will beat the steam drill."

The bet was made. It was the morning of the great race between John Henry and the steam drill. Polly Ann was wearing her best blue dress. She put their baby on the grass to watch his daddy.

John Henry's boss said to him, "Go on, beat that machine. I'll give you fifty dollars and a new suit!"

The people shouted, "John Henry, you can't beat that drill!"

John Henry answered, "Yes, I can!"

He walked slowly over to the mountain. The race was beginning! John Henry picked up his hammer. The metal arm of the steam drill went up and down. John Henry moved his hammer faster and faster. He pushed his steel bars slowly into the mountain. The steam drill pushed its bars into the mountain.

At the end of an hour the steam drill was beating John Henry.

By the end of the second hour John Henry finished as much as the drill. He worked very hard. His body was wet because he worked so hard.

The third hour John Henry was beating the drill. The people began to shout, "John Henry, beat the steam drill!"

The sun went down behind the mountains. A man shouted, "Stop. The race is finished. John Henry is the winner!" The people danced and shouted.

Suddenly they stopped. Everyone was quiet. John Henry smiled, but it was hard for him to breathe. He beat the drill, but his great heart was very tired.

Polly Ann put their son in John Henry's arms. He held up the baby. The baby put his little hands up to the stars. "You are very strong, my son." John Henry gave the baby back to Polly Ann. Then he died with his hammer in his hand.

They buried John Henry next to the railroad track. Every time a train goes by his grave, the train workers blow their whistles and say, "A great steel hero is buried over there."

Understanding the Story

A. What Happens?

Match the sentence parts. Write the correct letter in each blank.

_____ 1. The stranger showed   a. the drill, but his heart stopped.

_____ 2. He died   b. holes faster than four men.

_____ 3. John Henry can drill   c. their son in John Henry's arms.

_____ 4. Maybe it will kill me,   d. John Henry not to try.

_____ 5. Pretty Polly told   e. with his hammer in his hand.

_____ 6. John Henry beat   f. but I can beat the steam drill.

_____ 7. Polly put   g. a new machine to John Henry's boss.

B. Telling the Story Again

Fill in the blanks. Use the words you learned in **Practicing New Words**.

Americans remember how men built the _____s across America. Steel workers built _____s for the trains to ride through the mountains. They hammered _____s into the mountains. They took them out and put _____ in the holes to explode the rock.

    One day a man came to town to sell steam drills. John Henry's boss told him, "John Henry can _____ your drill!" The salesman made a _____ with John Henry's boss.

    One morning there was a great race between John Henry and the _____. John Henry worked for hours. He did not stop. At the end, it was hard for him to _____. He died with his _____ in his hand.

    The railroad company decided to _____ John Henry next to the railroad track. Everyone can remember this great American _____.

C. Looking Back

Answer these questions.

1. What job did John Henry have?
2. What did the salesman tell John Henry's boss?
3. What did John Henry say about the steam drill?
4. Who won the race?
5. What happened to John Henry?

Exploring the Meaning

A. Understanding John Henry's Life and Death

Complete the sentences in the chart. Then answer the question.

Before the Race	After the Race
John Henry says, "I'm a strong steel worker."	John Henry says, *"You are very strong, my son."*
John Henry is healthy.	John Henry
Polly Ann brings their baby to watch his daddy.	Polly Ann
John Henry	John Henry dies with a hammer in his hand.

Why did this strong, healthy worker die so young?

B. Thinking About the Story

Finish these sentences.

1. John Henry tried to beat the steam drill because he _____.

2. John Henry was a hero, but he made a mistake. He wanted to _____, but that is impossible.

3. John Henry's baby "put his little hands up to the stars." Like his father, the baby tried to reach

_____.

C. In Everyday Life

Talk about the following.

1. What problems do new machines make for workers?

2. What is a folk hero? Name some folk heroes in the history of your country.

3. Are most folktales completely true? How much of this story do you think is true? Which parts are probably not true?

The Princess of the Golden Island

POLISH

Poland is a large central European country. The language and people are Slavic. Until World War II most Polish people lived on farms. Today Poland has many factories, and many people live in large cities.

Before You Read

Talk about these questions.
1. Look at the picture for this story. Why is the girl playing a harmonica?
2. What stories do you know that have snakes in them?
3. Are you afraid of snakes? Why or why not?

Practicing New Words

You will find these words in the story. Study their meanings.

ant hill	a pile of earth made by ants
beak	the mouth of a bird
(to) complain	to say something is not good
courage	the ability to do something dangerous or frightening
evil	very bad; wanting to hurt other people
fairy	an imaginary person with magical powers
gravel	very small pieces of stone, sometimes used to cover streets
leader	a person other people follow
patience	the ability to do something or wait for something without getting angry or nervous
poppy seed	the tiny black seed of a poppy flower
(to) rule	to have power over
(to) separate	to take apart

Fill in the blanks with the new words. Use each word only once.

1. The man showed _____ when he jumped into the river to save the drowning girl.

2. Do you like to eat bread with _____s on top?

3. Good salespeople need to have lots of _____ with shoppers.

4. The new queen will _____ the country.

5. Who is the _____ of your country?

6. I think I will _____ to the store manager because this fruit is not good.

7. The workers put _____ on the street for cars to ride on.

8. In the story, a good _____ came to help the hardworking girl.

9. This bird uses its large _____ to pick up fish.

10. Look at the large _____ here in the field.
11. He had an _____ idea: to kill the princess and take her kingdom.
12. Please _____ the puzzle pieces and put them in the box.

The Princess of the
Golden Island

Long ago, the king and queen of the Golden Island died. Their little daughter, Majka, was left to rule the kingdom. She was only a child. The leaders had to choose someone to rule until she grew up.

The princess's uncle said, "I will rule the country until Majka grows up. Then she can rule." But the evil uncle secretly planned to keep the kingdom for himself.

He sent his servants to take care of Majka. An old man named Yust was his best servant. Yust had no love for anyone. He watched Majka day and night.

The servants dressed the princess in old clothes. They gave her terrible food. She got very little to eat. Her uncle wanted Majka to get sick and die. The princess was hungry and lonely, but she never complained. She was beautiful and good.

One day Yust fell asleep in the garden. He lay in between two ant hills. The big gray ants began to bite him. They were angry because the old man was in their way.

Majka saw the ants biting Yust. She pushed them away so the old man could sleep. Many of the ants bit her hands, but she stayed to protect the old man. When Yust woke up, he learned of Majka's kindness. Yust was surprised. He showed no love to Majka, but she was kind to him anyway. Her kindness won his heart.

Yust kissed the princess's hands. Then he gave her a small harmonica. He told her, "A good fairy gave this to me long ago. It has magic power, but only in the hands of a good person. Take it, child. In my hands it only plays. In your hands it will do magic."

122

When Majka played the harmonica, sweet sounds filled the air. Little animals jumped from the trees to listen. They wanted to be her friends. Birds flew to be near her.

Old Yust loved Majka, and she loved him. She called him "grandfather." Majka's uncle knew nothing about this. He was waiting for her to die. Yust told him, "She is getting thinner every day. Soon she will get sick and die." The uncle believed his servant.

The princess grew up. The leaders of the kingdom called a meeting. They said, "It is time for the princess to rule the country."

Majka's uncle was angry. "There is a law in our country," he said. "Anyone who wants to rule must show patience, courage, and love. Your princess must pass all three tests to become our ruler."

The day of the tests arrived. The princess entered the room. Her uncle said the first test was patience. "Here are many poppy seeds. They are mixed with gravel. You must separate the seeds from the gravel in one hour."

Everyone left the room. The little princess was alone. She began to cry. A large black bird flew in the window. She told him the problem. The bird flew out to the garden. "All birds, come to help! Help our little princess!" said the bird.

Many birds flew into the room and began to work. Their beaks picked the poppy seeds out of the gravel. They finished before the end of the hour. Then they flew away.

When the hour was over, the uncle and the leaders came in. They were very surprised! The poppy seeds and the gravel were separated. "I am happy to see your patience," Majka's uncle said angrily. "Now I will give you the test of courage."

He told the servants to bring in a box full of snakes. "Fight them," said the uncle. "In an hour we will return."

Majka looked at the snakes. They were ready to jump on her. The magic harmonica was on a table. She played a beautiful song on it. The snakes stood up like sticks and stopped moving.

The uncle returned in an hour with the other leaders. He was surprised and angry to find the princess alive. She was sitting in her chair. Around her were the snakes. None were moving.

"You won again," shouted the uncle. "Now comes the test of love, the last test. You must show the greatest love in the world."

How could the princess pass this test? The room was silent. Everyone was worried.

Majka fell at her uncle's feet. She said, "I love you, uncle! I love my father's brother with a true love. I give you the kingdom. I do not want to rule!"

The evil uncle could not believe his ears. He was so surprised that he fell dead on the floor.

In this way, Majka became the queen. She ruled the happy people of the Golden Island for many, many years.

Understanding the Story

A. When Does It Happen?

Put these sentences in the correct order. Write **1** next to the sentence that tells what happened first.

_____ Yust gave Majka a magic harmonica.

_____ Majka told her uncle she loved him.

_____ Majka's parents died.

_____ Majka protected the sleeping Yust from biting ants.

_____ The snakes stopped moving.

_____ The evil uncle died.

_____ The birds separated the seeds from the gravel.

_____ Majka got terrible food and clothes.

B. Telling the Story Again

Fill in the blanks. Use the words you learned in **Practicing New Words**.

A princess's parents died. She was a child and too young to _____. Her _____ uncle told the servants to give her a very hard life. He wanted her to die, so he could become king. Majka did not _____ about her hard life.

   Yust took care of her. One day he went to sleep between two _____s. The ants began to bite him, but Majka pushed them away. Yust and the princess became very good friends. He gave her a magic harmonica. It was a gift from a _____.

   When the _____s of the country said it was time for Majka to become queen, her evil uncle made her pass three tests. First she had to separate _____s from _____. This was a test of her _____. Many birds came to help her. They _____d the seeds from the gravel with their _____s.

   The second test was _____. The evil uncle put Majka in a room with dangerous snakes. She played the magic harmonica. The snakes stopped moving and did not attack her.

   The last test was love. Majka showed the greatest love when she told her uncle, "I love you. I give you the kingdom." The uncle was so surprised that he fell down dead. Majka became the queen of the Golden Island.

C. Looking Back

Answer these questions.

1. Why didn't Majka become queen when her parents died?
2. Why were the servants so bad to her?
3. Why did Yust give Majka the harmonica?
4. Why did her uncle give Majka three tests?
5. Why did the birds help Majka?
6. Why was her uncle angry?

Exploring the Meaning

A. Looking at the Three Tests

Complete the chart. Then answer the question.

Test	What the Uncle Thought	What Happened
one	*Majka could not separate the gravel from the seeds.*	
two		
three		

Why could Majka pass all of her tests?

B. Thinking About the Story

Finish these sentences.

1. Majka's life as a little girl was very sad because

   _____.

2. Her uncle wanted her to die because

   _____.

3. Majka got help from people and animals because she

   _____.

4. She finally became queen because

   _____.

5. Compare Majka to the "little orphan" in the Turkish story on pages 60–63. Both of them

   _____.

C. In Everyday Life

Talk about the following.

1. Do people always get rewards for doing good things? Explain your answer.
2. Think of a real child whose parent or parents died. Did the child's life change? How?
3. Think of a famous person in history who was evil. Did that person get what he or she wanted?

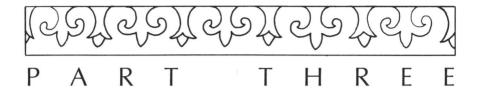

PART THREE

GETTING ALONG
with OTHERS

The Sun and the Moon

CUBAN

Cuba is an island in the West Indies, southeast of Florida. Cuba belonged to Spain for four hundred years. Spanish is still the main language of Cuba. Cubans grow a lot of cotton. They also grow tobacco and use it to make their famous Havana cigars.

Before You Read

Talk about these questions.

1. Find Cuba on a map of the world. Guess why it was one of the first countries to be controlled by the Spanish.

2. What stories do you know about the sun, moon, and stars? Why do many people make up stories about them?

Practicing New Words

You will find these words in the story. Study their meanings.

(to) catch up with	to reach
cave	a natural opening in a mountain
crowded	too full of people or objects
(to) get tired of	to not want to do any more (past: **got tired of**)
(to) hide	to put (oneself) in a secret place
lonely	a sad feeling because you are alone
plenty of	enough; lots of
(to) shine	to give light (past: **shone**)
(to) take turns	to do something one at a time, not together
the whole	all of the

Fill in the blanks with the new words. Use each word only once.

1. My grandmother spent _____ day in the hospital.
2. Some animals live inside a _____.
3. We have _____ food, so eat as much as you like.
4. The beautiful stars will _____ in the sky all night.
5. You can leave first. I'll _____ you in a few minutes because I walk faster than you do.
6. Call me on the telephone when you get _____.
7. Teachers _____ correcting papers every day.
8. Don't all talk at once! Please _____.
9. I don't want Sarah to see me. I'll _____ behind this tree.
10. On weekday mornings, the roads are often _____. Many people are driving to work at the same time.

The Sun and the Moon

The Sun and the Moon lived in a cave. No light of the Sun or Moon came out of the cave. Only the stars shone in the sky.

The Sun and the Moon got tired of living in the cave together. It was too crowded. The Sun said to the Moon, "I am the father of all life. It is not right for me to be together with you in a cave. Go away and leave this cave for me."

"Where can I go?" asked the Moon. "I have no other home," she said.

"Go into the sky," answered the Sun. "There is plenty of space for you in the big, blue sky."

The Moon was sad, but she left the cave. She was scared to be in the big, blue sky. She was only a thin, silver moon. She hid behind the clouds. Later she wasn't so scared. Little by little she showed her whole face. Everyone said it was beautiful.

The Sun saw the Moon in the beautiful, blue sky and got angry. The little Moon was in a better place than he was! He ran out of the cave and jumped into the sky.

When she saw the Sun coming, the Moon got scared and ran away. She kept looking back at the Sun. Soon nobody saw the Moon.

Now the Sun had the whole sky to live in. He sent his wonderful light in all directions. He warmed the cold Earth. Green plants and beautiful flowers began to grow. People danced and prayed to the Sun.

But the Sun was lonely. No one came near him. He had no one to talk to. The Sun wanted to find the Moon. The Sun went to look for her.

The Moon was hiding in the old cave. When the Sun came near the cave, the Moon ran out.

"Oh, Moon," shouted the Sun. "Where are you going? Why do you leave when I come near? Dear Moon, do not go away again!"

The Moon did not wait for the Sun. She went quickly into the sky. When the Sun came into the sky, the Moon left.

To this day the Sun cannot catch up with the Moon. Sometimes the Moon turns her cold face toward the Sun for a short time. Sometimes she turns her back on the Sun and passes quietly in front of him.

Now the Sun and the Moon take turns sleeping in the cave. Each day they travel separately through the sky.

Understanding the Story

A. When Does It Happen?

Put these sentences in the correct order. Write **1** next to the sentence that tells what happened first.

_____ The full Moon shone in the sky.

_____ The Moon hid behind the clouds.

_____ The Sun told the Moon to leave the cave.

_____ The Sun and the Moon traveled separately.

_____ The Sun and the Moon lived in a cave.

_____ The Sun and the Moon got tired of living together in a cave.

_____ The Sun got lonely.

_____ The Sun jumped into the sky.

B. Telling the Story Again

Fill in the blanks. Use the words you learned in **Practicing New Words**.

The Sun and the Moon lived together in a _____. It was _____ for the two of them in the cave. They _____ living together in the cave. The Sun told the Moon she had _____ space to shine in the sky.

    The Moon left sadly and _____ brightly in the sky. The Sun had _____ cave for himself: no one else was there. But he saw the Moon shining in the sky. He jumped into the sky, too. Then the Moon ran away. The Sun warmed the Earth, so plants grew everywhere. But the Sun got _____ because no one visited him. He wanted to _____ the Moon, but the Moon turned her face away. Now the Sun and the Moon _____ sleeping in the cave. They travel separately in the sky each day.

C. Looking Back

Answer these questions.

1. Why did the Moon leave the cave?

2. Why didn't the Moon want to leave?

3. Where did the Sun tell the Moon to go?

4. What happened when the Sun went into the sky?

5. Why did the Sun get angry after the Moon left the cave?

6. What did the Moon do every time the Sun came near her?

Exploring the Meaning

A. How the Story Explains Parts of Nature

Complete the chart. Then answer the question.

What Happens in the Sky	How the Story Explains It
The sun and the moon come in the sky at different times.	*The Sun and the Moon are angry with each other.*
We cannot always see the sun and the moon in the sky.	
Sometimes the moon looks thin.	*The Moon is scared. She is showing only part of her face.*
Sometimes the moon is "full."	
Some nights we can't see the moon: it's a "new moon."	*The Moon is turning her face toward the Sun, so we can't see it.*
Sometimes the moon hides the sun's light for a short time (a "solar eclipse").	
The sun and the moon seem to move across the sky.	

What is the purpose of this story?

B. *Thinking About the Story*

Finish these sentences.

1. The Sun and the Moon were unhappy together in the cave because _____.

2. The Sun told the Moon
   to _____.

3. Later, the Sun was lonely. He wanted to

   _____.

4. But now the Moon did not

   _____.

5. This story explains _____.

C. In Everyday Life

Talk about the following.

1. How do scientists explain the way the sun and the moon look and move?

2. How do scientists learn about things that happen in the sky?

3. Make up a story to explain another happening in nature, such as the changing of the seasons. Use your imagination.

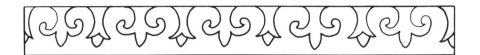

Urashima

JAPANESE

Japan is an Asian country made up of islands in the Pacific Ocean, east of China. In Japan, the old way of life of the Far East mixes with the modern clothing, movies, and music of the West. After World War II, Japan became a world leader in making cars, electronics, computers, iron, and plastics.

Before You Read

Talk about these questions.
1. What do you know about Japanese life and history?
2. Look at the picture of the boy in the boat. Guess why he is throwing the tortoise into the sea.
3. What do you know about protecting sea animals? What do they need protection from?

Practicing New Words

You will find these words in the story. Study their meanings.

beach	land near a lake or sea, often full of sand
bride	a woman getting married
cloud	a floating mass of water drops, smoke, or another light substance
coral	a hard, pink material made of skeletons of sea animals
emerald	an expensive, green stone
(to) float	to ride on top of water or air
forever	for all time; without end
line	a piece of string with a hook on one end and a pole on the other, used for fishing
pearl	a white material made by oysters inside their shells, often used in jewelry
ruby	an expensive, red stone
seashell	the hard covering of a sea animal, often found on the sand at a beach
wrinkled	covered with lines, often showing old age

Fill in the blanks with the new words. Use each word only once.

1. The _____ is wearing a beautiful white dress.

2. That _____ matches your green eyes.

3. Pieces of wood will _____ on water.

4. Look in that oyster shell for a _____.

5. A fish pulled on my _____.

6. Don't go to the _____ now. It is too hot.

7. I promise to love you _____!

8. I think it will rain. There's a big, black _____ in the sky.

9. My favorite stone is a _____ because I like red.

10. I want to buy that beautiful, pink _____ necklace.

11. People with _____ skin are usually old.

12. Sandra found a _____ on the beach.

Urashima

Many years ago a boy lived near the sea. His name was Urashima. He loved the water. One day he went fishing. Something pulled at his line. He brought it up. It was an old tortoise.

"I will not keep this old tortoise," said Urashima. "It still has many years to live." In Japan people believe that turtles live to be a thousand years old.

So the kind-hearted Urashima threw the tortoise back into the sea. He continued fishing. He fell asleep in the hot sun. Suddenly he heard a voice saying, "Urashima! Urashima!"

He looked up. Next to the boat was the tortoise.

The tortoise said, "Urashima, get on my back. You were kind to me, so I will take you to the Dragon King's palace."

Urashima got on its back and held on. The tortoise moved quickly across the water.

Soon they came to a magic island. It was filled with trees with emerald leaves and ruby fruits. Fish of all colors welcomed Urashima. They took him to a palace made of seashells and pearls, coral and emeralds. Inside the palace was a beautiful princess.

"Urashima," she said, "I was the tortoise who brought you here. I came to you in the form of a tortoise to test the kindness of your heart. Because you threw me back into the sea and did not sell me for food, I will give you a reward. I want to be your bride. You can live with me in this magic land and stay young forever. It is always summer here. Everything is always beautiful here."

Urashima was very happy to marry the beautiful princess. Together they drank from the wedding cup. Fish stood on their gold and silver tails and danced on the sand.

Urashima lived in happiness with the princess for three days.

Then he remembered his poor old father and mother. He wanted to see his family again. He wanted to see his village. "I must see my parents. It will be only for a day. Then I'll return to you, my dear wife," he said.

The princess did not want him to leave. She cried and said, "Go see your home, but take this box." She gave him a beautiful pearl box. "Take care of the box, and do not open it. If you open it, you can never return here."

Urashima got on a large tortoise. Soon he was on the beach near his home. He went into the village, but his father's house was gone. Everything looked strange. He did not know any of the people.

"Where is Urashima's house?" he asked an old man.

The old man looked surprised. "Urashima died three hundred years ago," he said. "He went fishing in his boat and never came back. Everyone in his family is dead now."

Urashima didn't know what to do. "I didn't stay three days. I stayed three hundred years. Everyone I know is gone!" he thought. "I can never see my family again. Now my only home is with the princess."

Urashima went back to the beach. He thought he heard his wife's voice calling him from the waves, but no tortoise came to carry him back to the Dragon King's palace.

Urashima looked at the little pearl box. "Maybe this will help me!" he thought.

Urashima forgot his promise to the princess. He opened the box. A little white cloud came out of the box. Urashima saw the face of the princess in the cloud. Then the cloud floated over the water.

Suddenly Urashima grew old. His hair turned white. His white beard blew in the wind. His skin became wrinkled. Soon he disappeared into the past, into the time when he lived. That night the beach was empty except for a little pearl box, shining in the moonlight.

Understanding the Story

A. *What Happens?*

Choose **a, b,** or **c** to complete each sentence.

1. Urashima threw the tortoise back into the sea because
    a. he did not like tortoise soup.
    b. he wanted the tortoise to live longer.
    c. he didn't know where to sell the tortoise.
2. Urashima wanted to see his parents because
    a. he was lonely for them.
    b. he was tired of living with the princess.
    c. they asked him to return.
3. When Urashima returned to his village,
    a. everything looked strange.
    b. it was good to be back home.
    c. his parents came to kiss him.
4. When Urashima opened the box,
    a. he grew old and died.
    b. a tortoise came to take him to the Dragon King's palace.
    c. the princess came to take him to the magic island.

B. *Telling the Story Again*

Fill in the blanks. Use the words you learned in **Practicing New Words**.

Once upon a time a fisherman named Urashima caught a tortoise. He threw it back into the sea because he knew the tortoise had many years left to live. Suddenly the tortoise returned. It took Urashima to the palace of the Dragon King.

When they got to the magic island, the tortoise turned into a princess. She wanted to be Urashima's _____ because he was so kind to the tortoise. Urashima and the princess lived in a beautiful palace made of _____s, pearls, pink _____, and _____s. It was possible to be young _____ in that magic land.

Urashima wanted to see his parents again. The princess gave him a _____ box to take with him. She told him not to open the box. Near his home, Urashima met an old man. He asked about his family. To his surprise, he discovered he was gone three hundred years. His family was dead.

Urashima wanted to return to the princess. He went to the _____. There was no tortoise waiting for him, so he forgot his promise and opened the box. Suddenly a _____ came out of the box. It began to _____ over the water. Urashima got old and died. Only the box was left on the sand.

C. Looking Back

Answer these questions.

1. Why did Urashima throw the tortoise back into the sea?
2. Why did the tortoise take Urashima to the Dragon King's palace?
3. Describe the magic island.
4. Describe Urashima's life on the magic island.
5. Why did Urashima return to his village?
6. What happened to Urashima on the beach?

Exploring the Meaning

A. Testing Main Characters

Complete the chart. It is about three stories in this book. Then answer the questions.

Character/Story	Urashima	The Princess of the Golden Island	The Little Orphan
What test(s) did he/she have?	*kindness, keeping a promise*	*patience, courage, and love*	*self-control*
Did he/she pass the test(s)?			
What was the reward?			

In what ways were these tests and their results the same? In what ways were they different?

B. Thinking About the Story

Finish these sentences.

1. Urashima showed kindness when he

   _____.

2. The magic island was different from the real world. In it

   _____.

3. Urashima got sad on the magic island. He wanted

   _____.

4. Urashima was surprised to learn that

   _____.

5. He could not return to the magic island because he

   _____.

6. Urashima got old and died because he forgot

   _____.

C. In Everyday Life

Talk about the following.

1. People face all kinds of tests in everyday life. Give examples of tests people face at home, at work, with friends, or on the street.
2. What is the most difficult test you ever faced (not at school)? Do you think you passed the test? What did you learn from it?
3. Did you ever forget a promise? What happened?

The Frogs and the Grubs

AUSTRALIAN

Australia is the only country that is a continent. Because it is completely in the Southern Hemisphere, people say it is "down under." The native people of Australia are called Aborigines. Today only a small number of Australians are Aborigines. Most Australians are people who came from Europe.

Before You Read

Talk about these questions.
1. What do you know about Australia's wild animals? Why are they different from animals in other countries?
2. Look at the picture for this story. What animals do you see?
3. What do you know about the Aborigines?

Practicing New Words

You will find these words in the story. Study their meanings.

(to) behave	to act in a good or bad way
(to) croak	to make the noise of a frog
dragonfly	an insect with large, transparent wings
(to) forgive	to pardon; not to be angry any more
grub	a wormlike baby insect
kangaroo	an Australian mammal with a pouch to hold its babies
mud	wet, soft earth
peacefully	without fighting
pond	a small lake
(to) punish	to make somebody pay for doing something bad
rainstorm	much rain and wind
(to) stir	to move around; to mix

Fill in the blanks with the new words. Use each word only once.

1. Look at the baby _____ in its mother's pouch.
2. Now the children are playing _____. Before they were fighting.
3. Don't _____ the child. He didn't know what he was doing.
4. Take your umbrella. There is going to be a big _____ today.
5. Can you _____ yourself better? Please act better!
6. Many animals come to drink at the _____.
7. I heard a frog _____ outside in the pond.
8. Clean your shoes before you come in. Don't bring in any _____.
9. Please _____ the soup so it doesn't burn.
10. Please _____ me for coming so late!
11. I found an insect in the earth. It's a _____.
12. A _____ has beautiful wings.

The Frogs and the Grubs

Once upon a time there was a beautiful pond. Many large trees and other plants grew around the pond. Many kinds of animals lived near the pond. There were kangaroos, rats, mice, geese, and birds of many colors. They all lived together peacefully.

One day there was a big rainstorm. It brought many frogs to the pond. They didn't like the other animals. The frogs decided to make the other animals unhappy. They wanted all the other animals to go away. They wanted the pond for themselves.

The frogs went down to the bottom of the pond and stirred up all the mud. This made the water taste bad. They also sang and croaked all night. No one could sleep.

All the animals asked the frogs to behave better. They did not listen.

One by one the animals and birds moved away. The beautiful pond was almost empty. Only the frogs and the grubs were left.

The sun loved to shine on this pond and on all the animals. He saw the frogs trying to kill the grubs that lived in the pond. This made him angry.

The sun decided to help the little grubs. He sent warm sunlight down on the grubs to make them strong. They grew strong enough to climb up the plants, out of the water. Then the sun made wings grow on the grubs' bodies. The wings were beautifully colored.

The sun decided to punish the frogs. He made it very hot around the pond. The water dried up. The plants died. Only a little mud was left.

The frogs were very uncomfortable. They were so thirsty they could not croak. In weak voices they asked the sun to be kind to them.

"You weren't kind to the other animals. They asked you not to make the water dirty. They asked you not to sing and croak so loudly at night," answered the sun. He shone down more on them.

Now the frogs were hungry and thirsty. They had nothing to eat. One by one, the grubs were changing into dragonflies and flying away from the pond.

Again and again the frogs asked the sun to forgive them. They promised they would behave better. They would never stir up the mud again. They would not eat the grubs that were left in the pond.

Finally the sun stopped punishing the frogs. He asked his friend the west wind to bring big rain clouds. It rained and rained. The pond filled with water.

Then the sun pushed away the empty clouds. He shone on the ground and brought all the plants to life. Soon everything was green again.

The animals heard the frogs' promises. They returned to the pond. Everyone was happy.

But to this day, the frogs sing and croak at night. No one can be good all the time!

Understanding the Story

A. What Happens?

Match the sentence parts. Write the correct letter in each blank.

_____ 1. The frogs didn't like   a. hungry and thirsty.

_____ 2. The frogs stirred up   b. the frogs.

_____ 3. All the animals asked   c. to behave better.

_____ 4. The sun saw   d. strong enough to climb
                                           up the plants.

_____ 5. The grubs grew   e. big rain clouds.

_____ 6. The sun punished   f. the frogs trying to kill
                                           the grubs.

_____ 7. The frogs were

_____ 8. The frogs promised

_____ 9. The west wind brought

g. the other animals.

h. the mud.

i. the frogs to behave better.

B. Telling the Story Again

Fill in the blanks. Use the words you learned in **Practicing New Words**.

Once there was a beautiful _____. Many kinds of animals lived _____ near the pond. One day a _____ brought many frogs to the pond. The frogs wanted all the other animals to go away, so they decided to _____ up all the mud. They also croaked all night, so the other animals couldn't sleep.

The animals asked the frogs to stop, but they didn't. Soon all the animals left except the frogs and the _____s.

The sun got angry, because he loved the animals. He saw the frogs trying to kill the grubs. He decided to help the grubs and to _____ the frogs for being bad. The sun made wings grow on the grubs. Every grub changed into a _____.

The frogs were very uncomfortable. They were too thirsty to _____. They asked the sun to _____ them. They promised to _____ better.

Finally the sun stopped punishing the frogs. He asked his friend the west wind to bring big rain clouds. It began to rain. The pond filled with water. The animals returned to the pond, and everyone was happy.

C. Looking Back

Answer these questions.

1. Why did the frogs stir up the mud and croak at night?
2. Why did the other animals leave the pond?
3. Why did the sun get angry?
4. How did the sun help the grubs?
5. How did the sun punish the frogs?

6. What did the frogs promise?
7. What happened at the pond after the rain came?

Exploring the Meaning

A. *Making Problems for Others*

Complete the chart. Then answer the questions.

Time	Which animals have problems?	What problems do they have?	Who made their problems?
beginning of story	*all the animals except the frogs*		
middle of story			

How does the sun punish the frogs for being bad to others? Is this a good punishment?

B. *Thinking About the Story*

Finish these sentences.

1. The frogs make problems for the other animals when they

  _____.

2. The other animals leave the pond because

  _____.

3. The sun teaches the frogs a lesson by

  _____.

4. Later the sun brings the animals back to the pond by

  _____.

C. In Everyday Life

Talk about the following.

1. Give examples of people or groups of people who act like the frogs.
2. How do you feel about those people? Why?
3. How can different kinds of people live together peacefully? What must they do?

The Great Peace

CANADIAN INDIAN

Canada is the second-largest country in the world in size. It has a small population because of its long, cold winters. The native people of Canada are the Indians and the Eskimos, or Inuit. People from France and England began moving to Canada in the 1600s and 1700s. Today Canada has two main languages: English and French.

Before You Read

Talk about these questions.
1. Look at the picture for this story. What are the people doing?
2. Why is it important for people to live in peace?
3. Did you ever live in a country that was at war? Why was it at war?

Practicing New Words

You will find these words in the story. Study their meanings.

celebration	a party
chief	the leader or head of a tribe
coast	land near the sea
contest	many people trying to win a prize
crown	something kings and queens wear on their heads
enemy	someone who hates or wants to hurt someone else
feast	a large, special meal
the Great Spirit	the power controlling everything in the world
tribe	many families that are related to each other
twins	two children born at the same time to one mother
war paint	paint some people put on their faces and bodies before going to war

Fill in the blanks with the new words. Use each word only once.

1. New York is on the _____ of the Atlantic Ocean.

2. Sometimes _____ look alike, but sometimes they look different.

3. The Queen of England has a beautiful gold _____.

4. Which _____ of Indians lives in this part of Canada?

5. We're having a _____ for Andy's birthday.

6. Canadian Indians prayed to _____ to help them.

7. We are cooking food for a _____ to celebrate making peace.

8. Please be my friend, not my _____.

9. Some North American Indians put _____ on their faces and bodies to bring them good luck in battle.

10. I hope I can win the writing _____.

11. The _____ of the tribe is talking to his people about the war.

The Great Peace

Once upon a time two tribes of Canadian Indians lived on the west coast of Canada. The Nootka tribe lived in the south. The Kwakiutl tribe lived in the north. The children of both tribes played on the beaches. Both tribes fished in the rivers and picked fruit in the valleys. Both tribes prayed to the Great Spirit.

The two tribes hated each other. They fought for the land. They killed each other. The land was full of anger.

A chief in the south had two beautiful daughters. They were twins. They did not hate anyone. They both spoke to the Great Spirit.

The little girls grew up into young women. Their father planned a feast to celebrate the change. He stopped the war for a few days. He told his people to prepare a great feast.

The girls were sad. They said, "It is good that our father is stopping the war to celebrate. But after the celebration he will fight again. Our hearts are tired of war."

They went to their father and said, "We are happy that you are making a great celebration. We want to sing and dance. But one thing is making us sad. We want the people in the north to come and be happy with us."

The chief was surprised. He said, "We are fighting them. We cannot celebrate with our enemies."

The girls looked very sad. One said, "Please do this for us, Father."

The chief loved his daughters. He sent people in boats to invite the tribe in the north to the celebration.

The people from the north put away their war paint and their bows and arrows. Men, women, and children came in their little boats.

They brought gifts and food for the feast. The children of

the two tribes played together. Everyone was happy. The two tribes ate together and told stories. There were songs, games, contests, and dancing. The celebration continued for many days.

At last they finished the food. The music stopped. The people from the north got into their little boats. "Good-bye, friends," they shouted.

The people from the south answered, "Good-bye, friends from the north." They watched them leave in their boats.

"Get our boats," said the chief. "We are going fishing."

"Aren't we going to start the war again?" asked the young men.

The chief answered, "There is no more war. We are going fishing."

So peace came to the land. People who laugh together cannot hate each other.

The Great Spirit wanted people to remember the good sisters. He turned them into twin mountains. The mountains have crowns of snow. They are high above the city of Vancouver. They give thanks forever for the blessing of peace.

Understanding the Story

A. When Does It Happen?

Put these sentences in the correct order. Write **1** next to the sentence that tells what happened first.

_____ The people from the north said good-bye.

_____ The Indian chief planned a feast.

_____ The two tribes ate together and played together.

_____ The tribe from the south went fishing.

_____ The two tribes fought for the land.

_____ The sisters became twin mountains.

_____ The twins asked their father to invite the enemy.

B. Telling the Story Again

Fill in the blanks. Use the words you learned in **Practicing New Words**.

Once upon a time there was a _____ of Canadian Indians on the western coast of Canada. They fought with another tribe that lived south of them on the _____.

The _____ of one of the tribes had two daughters. They were _____. He decided to make a _____ for them. They asked him to invite their _____. The chief was surprised at that idea, but he agreed. The people put away their _____. The other tribe came. They ate and played together. The two tribes had games and _____s in dancing and shooting. It was a wonderful _____.

After the other tribe left, the chief and his tribe went fishing. The war was finished. _____ wanted everyone to remember the two sisters. He turned them into two mountains. Each one has a _____ of snow. These mountains are near the city of Vancouver.

C. Looking Back

Answer these questions.
1. Why did the two tribes hate each other?
2. Why did the chief make a feast?
3. Why did the twins want to invite the enemy tribe?
4. Why did the chief agree to invite them?
5. What did the two tribes do together?
6. Why did the chief decide not to fight anymore with the other tribe?

Exploring the Meaning

A. Making War and Making Peace

Complete the chart. Then answer the question.

When?	What Did the Tribes Do?	Why?
before the feast		*Both tribes wanted the land.*
at the feast		
after the feast	*go home; go fishing*	

How did the lives of the tribes change because of the girls?

B. Thinking About the Story

Finish these sentences.

1. At the beginning of the story, the two tribes were

   _____.

2. The twins asked their father to

   _____.

3. The chief didn't want to _____.

4. When the other tribe came, they

   _____.

5. After the celebration, the chief told the young men that

   _____.

C. In Everyday Life

Talk about these questions.

1. Why do countries make war?
2. What countries are now at war? What are the wars about?
3. Is fighting a good way to solve problems? What are some other ways to solve problems?

David and the Spider

JEWISH

Jewish people live all over the world, but they are united by their four-thousand-year history and their religion. Hebrew is the historical language of the Jewish people. It is the main language of Israel today. This story is about David, who was king of Israel around 1000 B.C. It tells about David before he became king.

Before You Read

Talk about these questions.
1. Look at the picture for this story. What is the spider doing? What is the man doing?
2. What do you know about Jewish history?
3. Are you afraid of spiders? Why or why not?

Practicing New Words

You will find these words in the story. Study their meanings.

across   from one side to another

cave   a natural opening in a mountain

(to) chase   to run after; to try to catch

entrance   a door or opening

powerful   strong

(to) save   to keep safe; to protect

(to) shout   to speak very loudly

spider   an eight-legged animal (see picture)

(to) spin   to go back and forth to make a thread (past: **spun**)

(to) tear   to pull apart (past: **tore**)

ugly   not beautiful; bad-looking

web   a net of thin threads made by a spider to catch insects.

Fill in the blanks with the new words. Use each word only once.

1. Watch the dog _____ the cat up a tree!
2. It's cool and dark inside the _____.
3. A _____ storm is blowing over the city.
4. The nurse walked _____ the room.
5. Don't _____! I can hear you.
6. Every mother thinks her baby is beautiful. No mother thinks her baby is _____.
7. It is better to cut a paper than to _____ it.
8. An insect has six legs, but a _____ has eight.
9. A spider catches flies and other insects in its
_____.
10. A spider can _____ a beautiful web.
11. Where is the _____ to the building?
12. Thank you for pulling me out of the water.
You _____d my life!

David and the Spider

Once upon a time there was a powerful king named Saul.
He had many soldiers. One of them was David. David was a
brave soldier. He also sang beautiful songs. Saul loved David,
and David was always ready to help his king.

One afternoon David was in the palace garden. Everything
looked very pretty. David thought, "It is a beautiful world!"

Then David saw a spider in a tree. The spider was spinning
a web. David threw the spider on the ground. "You are ugly!"
he said. "Everything in this garden is beautiful except you.
You do no good in the world. You only spin webs."

David was ready to step on the spider. Suddenly he stopped.
"It is not your fault you are ugly and do no good in the world,"
he said sadly.

The spider's shiny black eyes looked at David. Then she ran
away. David went into the palace. He still thought that spiders
were the ugliest animals in the world. He was sure they were
not needed.

One day King Saul got very sick. He was sick in his mind.
His thoughts were all wrong. He did not love David any more.
He began to hate him. He thought David wanted to be king.

Saul told his soldiers to kill David. Saul's son was David's
friend. He told David what Saul said. David ran away before
the soldiers came to get him.

Saul was very angry. He and his soldiers looked everywhere
for David. For many days they chased David through the mountains. Often they were very close to him. One hot day David
came to a mountain full of many caves.

He went into a cool, dark cave to rest. Soon he fell asleep.
When he woke up, he heard Saul and his soldiers. "Look in
every cave!" Saul shouted.

David went far inside the cave to hide. He was afraid. He

heard the soldiers looking in the caves. Suddenly he saw a big, ugly spider. It was spinning a web across the entrance of his cave. The spider was going up and down, around and around, faster and faster. Her ugly body was making a beautiful web.

The soldiers were coming closer and closer. Then two men stood outside the cave. One of the men was Saul.

"This is the last cave," the soldier said to Saul. "I will go in and look for David."

The king told him, "You do not need to look in this cave. There is a spider web across the entrance. We can see that David did not go inside. The spider web is not broken."

Saul was suddenly very tired. He told his soldiers to stop and rest. Then he fell asleep at the entrance of the cave. The spider sat in the middle of her web and watched the king with her shiny little eyes. David hid at the back of the cave. He watched the spider in her web.

Later the king woke up. He left with his soldiers. David came out of the cave. He was happy to be alive.

David said to the spider, "I'm sorry, my friend. I tore your web when I came out of the cave. That little web saved me from the angry king. I'm sorry I said you do no good in the world. You saved my life!"

The spider did not answer. She only looked at him with her shiny black eyes. Then she ran away to make another web. David went away, too. He promised himself never again to say any animal has no use.

Understanding the Story

A. What Happens?

Chose **a, b,** or **c** to complete each sentence.

1. David did not step on the spider in the garden because
   a. the spider ran away.
   b. he couldn't catch the spider.
   c. it wasn't the spider's fault that she was so ugly.

2. King Saul wanted to kill David because
   a. David stole from him.
   b. David lied to him.
   c. he was sick in his mind.
3. David got away from King Saul because
   a. Saul's son told him that his father planned to kill him.
   b. Saul's soldiers told him to leave.
   c. Saul's son went with him.
4. The spider saved David because
   a. Saul's soldiers were afraid to go in the cave.
   b. Saul's soldiers thought no one was inside.
   c. Saul's soldiers were angry with Saul.
5. David asked the spider to forgive him for
   a. saying that spiders do no good in the world.
   b. saying that spiders are ugly.
   c. trying to step on her in the garden.

B. Telling the Story Again

Fill in the blanks. Use the words you learned in **Practicing New Words**.

David was a brave soldier. He was a soldier for Saul, a
_____ king. One day David was in the garden. He saw
a _____. David told the spider it was _____ and
did no good in the world.

   King Saul's mind got sick. Before he loved David; now he began
to hate him. He decided to kill him. David ran away. Saul told his
soldiers to _____ David and kill him.

   David went into a _____ to hide. Soon Saul's soldiers
were outside, looking for him. David saw a spider making a
_____. She was _____ the web
_____ the entrance to his cave.

   King Saul saw the spider web across the entrance of the cave. He
told his men not to enter the cave. He thought nobody was inside.
The spider web in the entrance _____d David.

   David told the spider he was sorry he _____ the
beautiful web to go outside. He understood his mistake. It was
wrong to say the spider does no good in the world. The spider
saved David's life.

C. Looking Back

Answer these questions.

1. Why did King Saul love David before he got sick?
2. What did David tell the spider in the garden?
3. Why did King Saul want to kill David?
4. Why did David go into the cave?
5. How did the spider save David's life?
6. What did David tell the spider after Saul left?

Exploring the Meaning

A. Getting Help from Nature

Complete the chart. It is about three stories in this book. Then answer the question.

Title of Story	Animals That Help	People Who Get Help	Reason for Help
David and the Spider			*to save him from Saul*
The Princess of the Golden Island		*Majka*	
Urashima	*tortoise*		

Why did the people in these stories get help from nature?

B. *Thinking About the Story*

Finish these sentences.

1. David does not understand that an ugly spider
   _____.

2. King Saul wants to kill David because he thinks that
   _____.

3. David goes into a cave to
   _____.

4. The spider hurries to spin a web to
   _____.

5. When King Saul and his men come to the cave, they
   _____.

6. David tells the spider he is sorry he
   _____.

C. *In Everyday Life*

Talk about the following.

1. The story tells us that the spider's "ugly body was making a beautiful web." Think of other examples when something ugly can change into something beautiful. Look at art, science, medicine, or any other part of life.

2. The story says that King Saul was "sick in his mind." How can a person who is sick in his mind become healthy again?

3. Do you think any animals are ugly? Why or why not? What makes something ugly?

The Sleeping Princess

MEXICAN

Mexico is in North America, south of the United States. The Aztecs, Mayas, and other native people of Mexico built great cities before the Spanish came in the 1500s. The Aztec city of Tenochtitlán is now Mexico City. More people live in Mexico City than in any other city in the world.

Before You Read

Talk about these questions.
1. What do you know about Mexican life and Mexican history?
2. Look at the picture of the prince and princess. Guess what will happen in this story.

Practicing New Words

You will find these words in the story. Study their meanings.

(to) accept	to agree to; to receive
(to) agree	to have the same opinion; to say yes
earthquake	a sudden shaking of the ground
excited	full of strong, happy feelings
handsome	good-looking
invader	someone from another place who comes to control your land
message	a piece of information
volcano	a mountain that sometimes has hot rock and steam coming out of it
(to) wander	to go without a plan or reason

Fill in the blanks with the new words. Use each word only once.

1. I am _____ about the party tomorrow!
2. The nurse gave the doctor my _____.
3. When steam begins to come out of a _____, get out of the way!
4. That _____ young man is my brother.
5. Will you please _____ my gift?
6. That strange-looking man is an _____ from another planet!
7. I don't _____ with you.
8. Everything shakes in an _____.
9. Hold your little boy's hand so he does not _____ away and get lost in the store.

The Sleeping Princess

Once a beautiful princess lived in the Aztec city of Tenochtitlán. Her father, the king, was a good and kind man. He told her, "You may choose the man you will marry. But he must be an Aztec prince."

The princess looked at the Aztec princes. She did not love any of them. Then one day a Chichimecan prince came to Tenochtitlán. The princess saw him on the street.

The young prince was tall and handsome. He saw the princess and looked into her eyes. The princess was excited. Here was the man of her dreams!

The prince finished his business and went home. He could not forget the beautiful Aztec princess. He wanted to see her again. He knew that the Aztec king would not let him meet his daughter. The Aztecs and the Chichimecans were enemies.

The prince sent a servant to Tenochtitlán with a message for the princess. The princess was happy. She loved the prince, and he wanted to see her!

Their servants helped them meet secretly. They met at night in the palace garden. The princess looked beautiful in the moonlight. The prince knew that he loved her.

The prince went home and wrote a letter to the Aztec king. He said he loved the princess and wanted to marry her.

The king called his daughter. "Did you meet this man?" he asked.

"Yes, I did. I love him," she said. "I want to marry him."

The king was very angry. He sent the princess to her rooms. She could not leave. Only the servants could go in.

Months passed. The princess's servants wanted to help her. They let the prince come into her rooms secretly. But the king learned about the prince's visits. He wanted to kill the prince.

At that time the Aztecs were fighting with another tribe. The king wrote to the prince. He asked for help in the war. "If your army helps us win the war, you can marry my daughter," he promised. The prince agreed.

The Chichimecans entered the war. Then the Aztec army stopped fighting. They left the Chichimecans alone to fight the other tribe. The king thought the prince and his small army would get killed. But the Chichimecans were very strong. They killed the enemy soldiers. They won the war for the Aztecs.

The king still would not let his daughter marry the prince. He told her that the prince died in the war. He told the prince that the princess got sick and died.

The prince did not believe the king. He learned that the princess was alive, but very sad. She thought her prince was dead.

The prince dressed like a farmer and went to Tenochtitlán. A servant let him enter the palace garden. He met the princess. They decided to run away and get married secretly. Then they would tell the king. Maybe he would finally accept the prince.

They followed their plan. When they returned to the palace, the king would not talk to them. He sent them away and made a law: No one in the Aztec nation could give them food or a place to sleep.

The prince and the princess wandered from place to place. They were hungry and cold. After many months, they found a small valley far from Tenochtitlán. Here they lived by themselves for many years.

One day the princess became very sick. For weeks the prince cared for her. She did not get well. One night the great god of the mountains spoke to the prince. "My son, this is your loved one's last night in this life. But do not be afraid. She will not die. She will fall into a deep sleep. In many years, strange people will come to the Aztec land. You will wake the princess with a kiss and push the strangers out of this valley."

The voice stopped. The prince and princess talked about their love and about the promise of the gods. The princess kissed her husband and fell asleep in his arms. Then a great earthquake shook the valley. Two volcanoes rose up. Fire and smoke filled the sky.

The voice spoke again. "Take the princess to the top of the northern mountain. Then go to the top of the southern mountain to watch her. We will call you when it is time to wake the princess and push out the invaders."

The prince did as the gods told him. Snow covered the two lovers. But the gods keep the mountaintop fires burning to this day, like the never-ending love of the prince and his sleeping princess.

Understanding the Story

A. *What Happens?*

Match the sentence parts. Write the correct letter in each blank.

_____ 1. The prince helped   a. the prince come secretly into the garden.

_____ 2. The king said   b. two snow-covered mountains.

_____ 3. The servants helped   c. the Aztecs win the war.

_____ 4. The princess fell in love   d. together to get married.

_____ 5. The prince and the princess became   e. no one could help the couple.

_____ 6. The couple ran away   f. with a Chichimecan prince.

_____ 7. The king wanted   g. his daughter to marry an Aztec prince.

_____ 8. The princess fell asleep   h. in her husband's arms.

B. Telling the Story Again

Fill in the blanks. Use the words you learned in **Practicing New Words**.

A beautiful Aztec princess fell in love with a _____ young Chichimecan prince. She was _____ to see the man she dreamed about. He fell in love with her, too, and wanted to marry her. Her father did not _____ to that. He would not _____ a Chichimecan as a son.

The king sent a _____ to the prince. He said the prince could marry the princess if he helped the king win a war. The prince did that, but the king still did not want him to marry the princess. Finally the couple decided to run away and marry. They had to _____ from place to place, looking for food.

One day the princess got sick and fell asleep in her husband's arms. An _____ shook the valley. The prince and princess each went up to the top of a snow-covered _____. The volcanoes stand side by side. They continue to burn like the never-ending love of the prince and his sleeping princess.

C. Looking Back

Answer these questions.

1. What did the king tell the princess?
2. What man did she fall in love with?
3. What did the king do when he heard about the Chichimecan prince?
4. What message did the king send to the prince?
5. What did the king do after the prince and his army won the war?
6. What did the prince and the princess decide to do?
7. What happened to the princess?
8. What do the Mexican people have in their land to remind them of the prince and the princess?

Exploring the Meaning

A. *Finding the Right Husband*

Complete the chart. It is about three stories from this book. Then answer the question.

Story	Main Character	Country	Person She Marries	Reason
The Sleeping Princess	*the Aztec princess*			*they love each other*
The Land of the Blue Faces		*China*		
Why the Monsoon Comes Each Year			*the mountain god*	

In these stories, who chooses a husband for a princess?

B. *Thinking About the Story*

Finish these sentences.

1. The king wanted the princess to marry an Aztec, but
   _____.

2. The princess fell in love _____.

3. Her father didn't want her to see the prince, so he
   _____.

4. The king tricked the Chichimecan prince into
   helping _____.

5. The couple decided _____.

6. Their life together ended when
   _____.

7. Two volcanoes remind the people of
   _____.

C. In Everyday Life

Talk about these questions.

1. In your country, do parents choose the person their child will marry? Do young people decide for themselves?

2. In your opinion, should parents choose the person their child will marry? Should young people marry anyone they fall in love with? Why or why not?

3. Do you know a story about a mountain, river, or other place in your country?

A Jar of Olives

ARAB

*The Arab language and culture are found all over the world,
but most Arabs live in the Middle East (southwestern Asia)
and northern Africa. Most Arabs are Muslim. Their holy
city, Mecca, is in Saudi Arabia.*

Before You Read

Talk about these questions.
1. This story is from *The Thousand and One Nights*, also called
   The Arabian Nights. Do you know the stories of Aladdin, Ali
   Baba, and Sinbad?
2. What do you know about the life and climate of the Middle
   East and North Africa?
3. Look at the picture for this story. What is the man doing?

Practicing New Words

You will find these words in the story. Study their meanings.

caravan	a group of people traveling together for safety
chief justice	the head of the courts in a country
expert	a person who knows a lot about a subject
goods	things to buy or sell
holy	having to do with God or religion; having special religious meaning
jar	a container that can be closed at the top to keep air out
(to) join	to become part of
(to) load	to put things on or in
mosque	a house of prayer for Muslims
(to) pretend	to make believe something that isn't true; to imagine
spoiled	not good to eat; ruined

Fill in the blanks with the new words. Use each word only once.

1. Please buy a _____ of coffee at the supermarket.
2. Do you want to _____ the art club?
3. That meat is _____ because it wasn't in the refrigerator.
4. Here are the suitcases. Will you please _____ the car?
5. A _____ of travelers is going across the desert.
6. Children often _____ they are doctors, fire fighters, or princesses.
7. That professor is an _____ in Arab history, especially the Ottoman empire.
8. Arabs go to their _____ on Fridays to pray.
9. The _____ explained the new law to the people.
10. The truck driver is taking the _____ off his truck to give to the shopkeeper.
11. My friend wants to visit the _____ city of Mecca.

A Jar of Olives

Ali Cogia was a Muslim businessman. He lived in Baghdad. Ali decided to visit the holy city of Mecca. Every good Muslim should go to Mecca once in his lifetime.

Ali Cogia had one problem. He had a thousand pieces of gold. He wanted to leave them in Baghdad. Where would they be safe?

Ali put the money in the bottom of a jar. He filled the jar with olives. He carried the jar to a friend. Ali said to his friend, "My brother, I am going to Mecca. Will you keep this jar of olives for me until I come back?"

His friend was also a businessman. He said, "Put the jar in my shop. I promise you will find it in the same place when you return."

A few days later, Ali Cogia loaded his camel with goods to sell on the trip. He joined a caravan. He arrived in Mecca and visited the Holy Mosque. Then he joined a caravan to Cairo. In Cairo, he sold all his goods and bought some Egyptian goods. He went to Damascus for a few weeks. There he sold the Egyptian goods. Ali visited friends in Persia and India. He was gone for seven long years.

One day the friend's wife said, "I'm hungry for some olives."

The businessman said, "Seven years ago Ali Cogia went to Mecca. He left a jar of olives here. I promised to take care of it for him. He never came back. He must be dead. We can eat those olives."

His wife answered, "No. Don't touch the jar! We have no news about Ali Cogia. That does not mean he is dead. What if he comes back? He will find out that you did not keep your promise. You will feel terrible! I don't want any olives. They are probably spoiled."

But her husband didn't listen. He went to his shop and found the jar. He opened it. The olives on top were spoiled. He wanted to see if the ones on the bottom were also spoiled. The businessman found the gold pieces under the olives. He was very surprised. He put everything back in the jar and returned to his wife.

"You are right," he told her. "The olives are spoiled. I put them back. Ali Cogia will never know I touched his jar."

All night the friend thought about the gold in the jar of olives. The next morning he took the gold and hid it. He threw away the old olives and bought new olives. He filled Ali Cogia's jar with the new olives. Then he put the jar back where Ali left it.

A month later Ali Cogia returned to Baghdad. He went to get the jar of olives from his friend. When he put his hand into the jar, he found only olives. He cried out, "Could my friend steal from me?"

Ali's friend pretended not to know about the gold. He said, "You asked me to keep a jar of olives for you. Now you say there was gold in the jar? What a story!"

Ali Cogia and his friend told their stories to a judge. The judge believed Ali's friend. He said the friend did not take the gold. Ali was very angry.

Ali went to the chief justice. The justice agreed to hear the story the next day. That night the justice took a walk. He saw some children playing outside. They knew the story of Ali Cogia and his jar of olives. The justice listened to their game.

"Let's pretend that I am the judge," said one boy. "Bring Ali Cogia to me." Another child pretended to be Ali Cogia. A third played the friend. "Ali Cogia" and the "friend" told their stories to the "judge." Then the boy playing the judge shouted, "I want to see the jar of olives!" "Ali Cogia" pretended to bring the jar. The "judge" said, "I want to taste the olives. Oh, they are excellent. Why do old olives taste so good? Find some olive experts."

Two more children pretended to be the olive experts. They said, "Olives are good for three years. After that, they lose both taste and color." The "judge" showed the "experts" the jar of olives. They said, "These olives are fresh. They cannot be seven years old."

The "judge" said to the boy playing Ali, "Your friend lied. He is a thief."

The chief justice was surprised. The children were very wise! He invited the boy who played the judge to come to his court the next day.

The next day the chief justice and the little boy listened to Ali Cogia and his friend. Then they asked for the jar of olives and two olive experts. The experts said, "These olives are fresh. They cannot be seven years old."

The businessman finally told Ali Cogia where he hid the gold. Then the guards took him away and punished him.

The chief justice sent the little boy home with a hundred pieces of gold in his pocket. "The truth comes from the mouth of a child," he said.

Understanding the Story

A. When Does It Happen?

Put these sentences in the correct order. Write **1** next to the sentence that tells what happened first.

_____ Ali Cogia's friend said he didn't take the gold.

_____ Ali Cogia decided to visit the Holy Mosque in Mecca.

_____ The chief justice heard some children playing "Ali Cogia."

_____ The judge decided Ali Cogia's friend didn't take the gold.

_____ Ali Cogia put some gold inside a jar of olives and gave it to his friend.

_____ The chief justice gave the little boy a hundred pieces of gold.

_____ Ali Cogia's friend took the gold out of the jar of olives.

_____ Ali Cogia returned home and found no gold in the jar of olives.

_____ The businessman told Ali Cogia where he hid the gold.

_____ Ali Cogia joined a caravan to Mecca.

B. *Telling the Story Again*

Fill in the blanks. Use the words you learned in **Practicing New Words**.

A Muslim businessman named Ali Cogia lived in Baghdad. He decided to go to the Holy _____ in Mecca. He wanted to hide a thousand pieces of gold in Baghdad before he left. He put the gold in a _____ of olives and left it with a friend. The friend promised to take good care of the jar until he returned.

Ali Cogia _____ed everything on his camel. Then he _____ed a _____ going to Mecca. He went from place to place and stayed away for seven years. He sold his _____ in many countries.

Ali's friend did not touch the jar all that time. Then one day his wife wanted to eat some olives. Ali Cogia's friend opened the jar and found _____ olives at the top and gold at the bottom. He hid the gold and put fresh olives in the jar.

A month later Ali Cogia returned. He looked for the gold in the jar, but it was gone. His friend _____ not to know about the gold.

Ali Cogia and his friend went to a judge. The judge believed the friend. Ali was angry. He decided to tell the _____ his story. The night before he heard the story, the chief justice saw some children playing "Ali Cogia." One of the children said Ali's friend took the gold because the olives in the jar were fresh. This helped the chief justice understand the truth. He asked two olive _____s to look at the olives. They said the olives were fresh. This proved Ali's friend lied. He told Ali where he hid the gold. The chief justice punished the thief and gave the smart little boy some gold.

C. *Looking Back*

Answer these questions.

1. Why did Ali Cogia go to Mecca?
2. Where did Ali hide a thousand pieces of gold?
3. What did he do with the jar of olives?

4. What did the friend promise?
5. Why did Ali Cogia go to the chief justice?
6. What did the chief justice learn from a child?

Exploring the Meaning

A. Asking for Help

Complete the chart. It is about four stories in this book. Then answer the question.

	A Jar of Olives	One More Child	The Tortoise Wins a Race	Mr. Frog's Dream
Culture	Arab			
Who needs help?		the rich woman		
What is the problem?			the tortoise needs to win a race	
Who helps?		her friend		two ducks
Does the help solve the problem?	no			

Do friends always give good help? Why or why not?

B. *Thinking About the Story*

Finish these sentences.

1. Ali Cogia thought that his friend

   _____.

2. He was gone a long time because he

   _____.

3. The friend didn't keep his promise because

   _____.

4. Ali Cogia had to go to the chief justice because

   _____.

5. The chief justice learned that some children

   _____.

6. At the end of the story, _____.

C. *In Everyday Life*

Talk about these questions.

1. Did you ever ask a friend for help? What happened?
2. Do you have a friend who needs your help? How can you help?
3. What kinds of changes can you expect when you leave home and then return after a long time?

The Giants and the Dwarfs

DUTCH

The Netherlands is a small country in northwestern Europe.
It is often called Holland. The people and language are
called Dutch. The Netherlands is on the North Sea, and
much of its land is below sea level. The Dutch work hard to
keep the sea out of their low land.

Before You Read

Talk about the following.

1. Holland is famous for its windmills, dikes, wooden shoes, and
   tulips. How do the Dutch use windmills and dikes to keep the
   sea out of their land?

2. Look at a map of the Netherlands. Guess why this country was
   once a great sea power.

3. Look at the picture for this story. Guess why the dwarfs are dancing around the fire.

Practicing New Words

You will find these words in the story. Study their meanings.

(to) dig	to make a hole in the ground (past: **dug**)
dwarf	a very small person
fireplace	a place in a house to build a fire
giant	a very tall person
huge	very large
(to) knock down	to push down
(to) lock	to close so a person can only enter with a key
mole	a small, furry animal that digs tunnels
root	the bottom part of a tree, in the earth
(to) snore	to make noise when asleep
spark	a tiny bit of fire
weed	a plant that is not wanted, but grows by itself

Fill in the blanks with the new words. Use each word only once.

1. Don't forget to _____ the door.
2. When you _____ I cannot sleep!
3. There are two _____ trees in front of the school.
4. A little _____ is digging tunnels in my garden.
5. Don't run on the sidewalk. You might _____ people walking there.
6. I work hard in my garden, so I don't have any _____s.
7. A _____ can be a good basketball player.
8. I know a story about a _____ who lives in a little box.

9. A _____ from a fire burned down thousands of trees.

10. Long ago people heated their houses and cooked in a _____.

11. Before you plant a rose, you must _____ a hole.

12. Put lots of water in the hole so that all the _____s get wet.

The Giants and the Dwarfs

Once upon a time three giants came to the hills of Gelderland. No one knew where they came from. The giants were always happy. They played and chased each other all day. The ground shook under their huge feet.

Many dwarfs lived in these hills. They had tunnels and rooms under the ground. They were afraid of the giants. When a giant came running in their direction, the dwarfs ran away quickly and hid in their holes.

When the giants were tired, they lay down to sleep on the hillside. They snored so loudly that the dwarfs could not sleep in their holes.

They were not bad giants. When they were sleeping, smiles came on their beautiful young faces. This only happens to people who are good and happy.

One day the oldest giant said to his brothers, "This is a beautiful country. Let's build a house and live here." The other giants agreed. The happy giants cut down trees and moved rocks. By evening their home was ready.

That night the dwarfs did not sleep at all. Hundreds of them met in the moonlight in an open field. The dwarfs talked about their problem.

"Friends, we must send away these giants," said a dwarf man. "They walk above our homes with their big feet. Our houses will fall in! They snore so much at night that we cannot sleep. There is only one thing to do. We must knock down their house."

A dwarf woman disagreed. "We should talk to them. We can explain our problem. Maybe they will stay away from our homes. Then we can live together in peace."

The other dwarfs shouted, "What does a woman know? Men know better! Woman, go home! Work in your kitchen!"

So the dwarfs tried to knock down the house. They worked all night. By morning they made a few little holes around the house.

"There must be rabbits around here," said one giant. He stamped his foot and filled in the holes with some dirt.

That night the dwarfs met again. One said, "Last night we tried to knock down the giants' house. We weren't strong enough. But we can steal some fire from their fireplace. We can use the fire to burn down their house!"

"How can we get in?" asked another dwarf.

"We'll dig a tunnel under the house to the fireplace," answered a third.

The dwarfs started to work. They dug and dug, but the noise of the snoring giants knocked down their tunnels. They started over many times. Finally they all ran away.

The next day the giants said, "There must be moles under our house. Look at the tunnels here." They threw dirt in the holes and covered their floor with rocks.

That night the three giants sat around their fireplace. They talked about their plans. "We will plant potatoes and other crops," they said. "We'll plant more trees, too." Their door was open. The dwarfs stood outside. They looked in and listened to the giants talking.

When the giants went to bed, they forgot to lock the door.

Suddenly one of the giants woke up. He smelled fire. The room was full of smoke. Everything was burning! He woke his brothers. They all ran out of the house. A minute later the burning house fell down.

The dwarfs laughed and danced in a circle around the burning house. The giants were too big to see them. They sat sadly looking at the big fire.

The giants said, "We forgot to lock the door. The wind probably blew sparks from the fireplace to start the fire. Tomorrow we must build a new house. We'll build three houses. If one burns down, we'll have two more."

In the morning they started to build. The dwarfs watched. By evening the giants finished one house. By the end of the week they had three. At night they locked the doors. In the daytime they planted crops and sang happy songs.

The dwarfs put weeds in the fields. The three giants pulled the weeds. The giants planted trees on top of the hill to protect their houses from the wind. The dwarfs dug under the trees and cut the roots. When one tree died, the giants planted two more. Soon the trees were very strong. Their roots were too big for the dwarfs to cut.

What finally happened? The dwarfs could not make the giants leave. They had to live with them. The dwarfs moved their homes. They built new tunnels and rooms in places where the giants did not walk.

The three giants planted more trees and crops. Everything grew well. Years passed. People named the place "Three." To this day the strong trees stand on the hill. Nothing can hurt them. The giants planted them.

Understanding the Story

A. What Happens?

Choose **a, b,** or **c** to complete each sentence.

1. The dwarfs were afraid of the giants because
   a. they snored.
   b. they were bad.
   c. they were so big.

2. The dwarfs decided to
   a. move away from the giants.
   b. talk to the giants about their problems.
   c. knock down the giants' house.

3. What did the dwarf men say to the dwarf woman?
   a. They said she didn't know anything.
   b. They said she had a good idea.
   c. They said she snored.

4. At their second meeting, the dwarfs decided to
   a. move away.
   b. talk to the giants.
   c. burn down the giants' house.

5. The dwarfs tried everything to make the giants leave except
   a. talking to the giants.
   b. putting weeds in their fields.
   c. cutting the roots of the giants' trees.

6. The dwarfs finally had to
    a. live with the giants.
    b. talk to the giants.
    c. run away from the giants.

B. Telling the Story Again

Fill in the blanks. Use the words you learned in **Practicing New Words**.

In the hills of Gelderland there were three _____
men. They were _____s, happy men with big feet.
They were good men. Under the hills lived many _____s.
They got angry when the giants began to _____ every night.
    The dwarfs tried many tricks to make the giants go away. First
they tried to _____ their house. They _____
tunnels around it. The giants thought there were rabbits or
_____s nearby. When the giants forgot to _____
the door of their house, the dwarfs stole a _____ of
fire from their _____ and burned down their house.
    Next the giants built three new houses and planted crops. The
dwarfs put _____s in their fields. They tried to cut the
_____s of every tree the giants planted, but they
could not. Every time the dwarfs did something bad to them, the
giants worked hard and solved the problem. The dwarfs finally had
to learn to live with the giants, and they did.

C. Looking Back

Answer these questions.

1. What kind of people were the giants?

2. What kind of people were the dwarfs?

3. What did the dwarfs do to the giants? Why did they do these
   things?

4. What did the dwarf woman want to do?

5. Why didn't the dwarf men try her idea?

6. What did the dwarfs finally have to do?

Exploring the Meaning

A. *Solving Problems*

Complete the chart. Then answer the question.

Who?	What Problem Did They Have?	What Did They Do?
the dwarfs	giants came to their hills	*tried to make them leave*
	the giants built a house	tried to knock it down
the dwarfs	they couldn't knock down the giants' house	
the giants		built three new houses
the dwarfs	the giants planted crops	
the giants		pulled the weeds
	the giants planted trees	cut the roots to make the trees die
the giants	their trees died	

Who was better at solving problems: the giants or the dwarfs? Why?

B. Thinking About the Story

Finish these sentences.

1. The giants worked to _____.
2. The dwarfs worked to _____.
3. The dwarf men should learn that women

   _____.

4. The dwarfs learned that sometimes you have to

   _____.

C. In Everyday Life

Talk about the following.

1. What is the best way to solve problems with neighbors?
2. Why should men and women listen to each other's ideas?
3. Think of a problem you had with someone. Did you solve it? If so, how? If not, why not?
4. Can all problems be solved? What should you do if you have a problem you can't solve?